1978

1978

PEOPLES OF THE EARTH

volume eight

The Pacific

Micronesia and Polynesia

THE DANBURY PRESS

(Previous page) As the sun
passes below the Pacific
horizon, Tahitian fishermen lure
encircled fish to the surface
with torches, and then net them.

Editorial Director **Tom Stacey**

Picture Director **Alexander Low**
Executive Editor **Katherine Ivens**
Art Director **Tom Deas**
Assistant Editor **Elisabeth Meakin**
Project Co-ordinator **Anne Harrison**
Research **Cheryl Moyer**

Specialist Picture Researcher **Claire Baines**
Picture Research **Elly Beintema**
Diana Eggitt
Jeanne Griffiths
Emma Stacey
Editorial Assistants **Richard Carlisle**
Rosamund Ellis
Minette Marrin
Susan Rutherford
Xan Smiley
Design Assistants **Susan Forster**
Richard Kelly
Cartography **Ron Hayward**
Illustrations **Sandra Archibald**
Ron McTrusty

Production **Roger Multon**
Production Assistant **Vanessa Charles**

The DANBURY PRESS
a division of GROLIER ENTERPRISES INC.
Publisher
ROBERT B. CLARKE

© 1973 Europa Verlag

Library of Congress Catalog Card No. 72 85614

Printed in Italy by
Arnoldo Mondadori Editore, Verona

The publishers gratefully acknowledge help from
the following organizations:
Royal Anthropological Institute, London
Musée de l'Homme, Paris
International African Institute, London
British Museum, London
Royal Geographical Society, London
Scott Polar Research Institute, Cambridge
Royal Asiatic Society, London
Royal Central Asian Society, London
Pitt-Rivers Museum, Oxford
Horniman Museum, London
Institute of Latin American Studies, London

Contents

Supervisory Editor of the Series:
Professor Sir Edward Evans-Pritchard,
Fellow of All Souls, Professor of Social Anthropology,
University of Oxford, 1946-1970,
Chevalier de la Légion d'Honneur

Volume Editor:
Dr John Clammer, Department of Sociology
and Social Anthropology, University of Hull,
author of *Literacy and Social Change in
Fiji* etc.

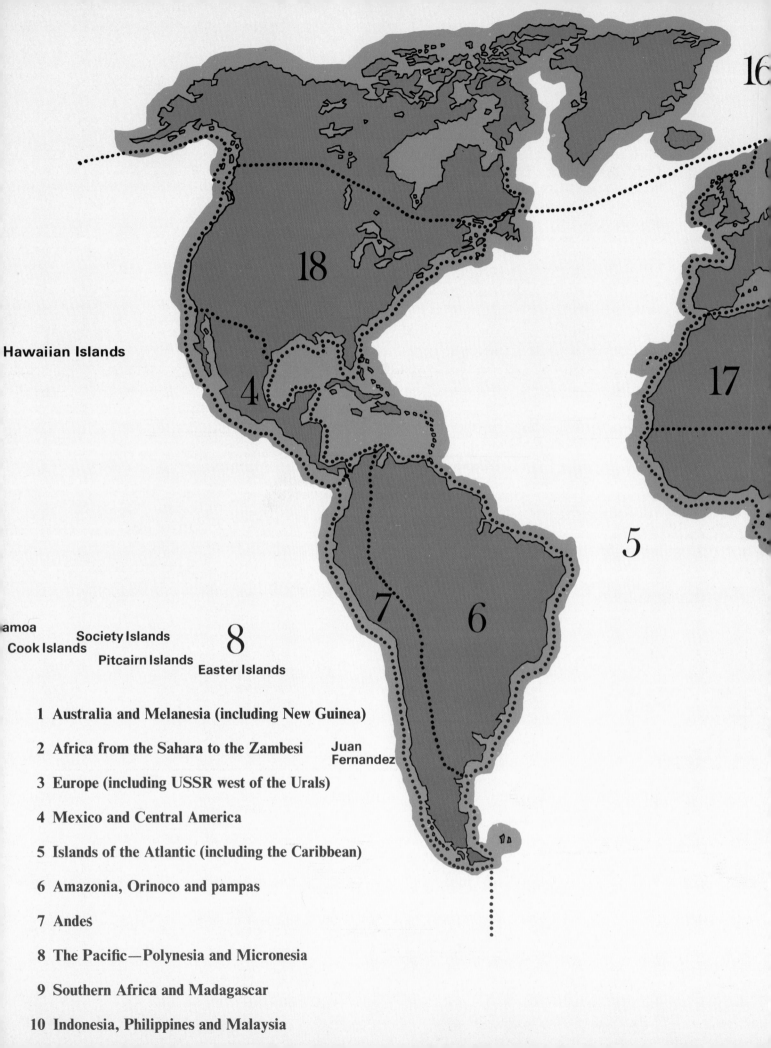

16

Hawaiian Islands

18

4

17

5

amoa
Cook Islands
Society Islands
Pitcairn Islands
8
Easter Islands

7 6

Juan
Fernandez

1 Australia and Melanesia (including New Guinea)

2 Africa from the Sahara to the Zambesi

3 Europe (including USSR west of the Urals)

4 Mexico and Central America

5 Islands of the Atlantic (including the Caribbean)

6 Amazonia, Orinoco and pampas

7 Andes

8 The Pacific—Polynesia and Micronesia

9 Southern Africa and Madagascar

10 Indonesia, Philippines and Malaysia

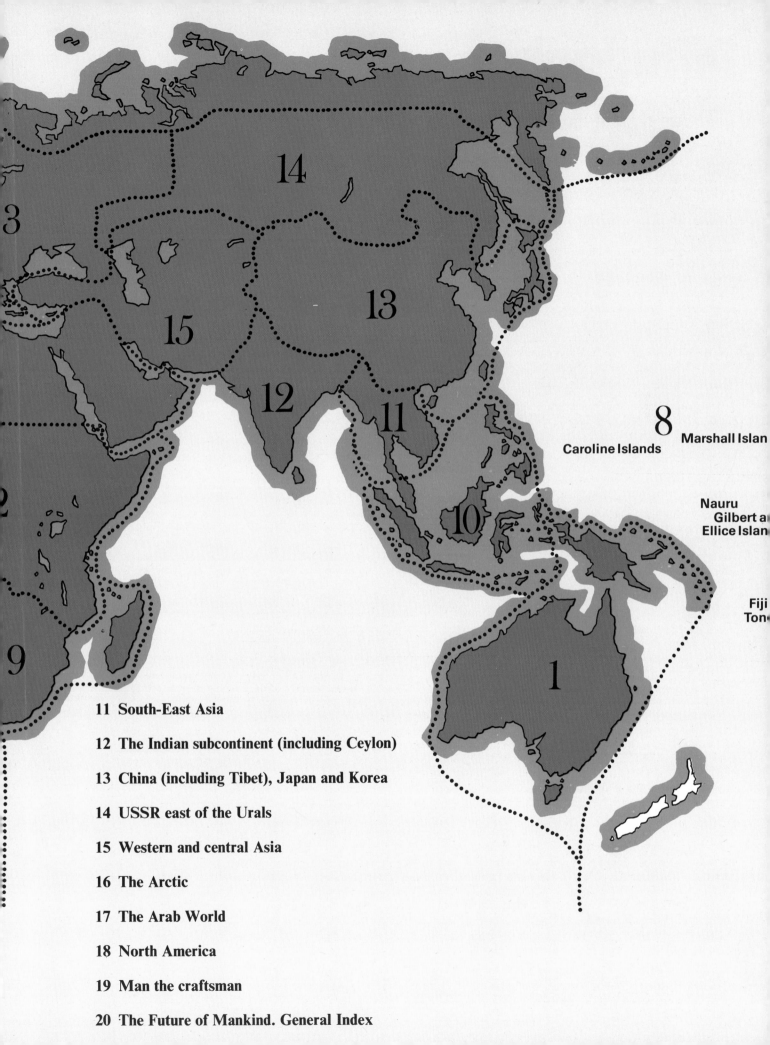

3

14

13

15

12

11

8

Caroline Islands

Marshall Islan

Nauru
Gilbert a
Ellice Islan

10

Fiji
Ton

2

9

1

Diffusionism: the spread of cultures

Speculations as to contacts between the Old World and the New before the voyages of Columbus are unceasing. But as archaeologists and anthropologists unfold the secrets of the past, these speculations have become polarized into two opposing schools of thought: isolationism and diffusionism. The isolationists believe that the two main oceans surrounding the Americas completely isolated the New World from Old World contact until Columbus' voyage in 1492; this school of thought allows only for the movement of food-gatherers across from the Siberian tundra to Alaska in America's arctic north. These were America's first immigrants until the 15th century. From them evolved the North American Indian societies, and the more sophisticated societies of South and Central America – the famous Incas and Aztecs. To isolationists, the oceans were enormous, dead, immobile lakes; barriers to human movement in any direction.

In contrast, the diffusionists believe in a common cradle for the Old World civilizations and those of the New World. They postulate various voyages from Asia, Europe or Africa in pre-Columbian times, regarding the oceans almost as open 'skating rinks' across which aboriginal voyagers could travel in any direction they wished. Among extreme diffusionists and isolationists alike, there appears the same disregard for oceanographic factors like winds and currents. Without an appreciation of how these decisive factors would affect ancient voyagers, the theorizing of either school of thought becomes valueless. Whatever the parallels between Old and New World civilizations, there can be no certainty of any contact until the means of contact is proved possible.

Isolationists and diffusionists agree that there are many, often remarkable, similarities between the advanced civilizations of pre-Columbian America and those of the ancient Mediterranean world. But these similarities are interpreted in very different ways. Isolationists suggest that parallels and occasional identical occurrences can be ascribed to independent evolution along parallel lines. This is based on the knowledge that the human mind tends to react inventively in a similar way to similar challenges on either side of a geographical barrier – in this case, the Atlantic and Pacific oceans. Ideas and inventions, customs and cultural traits found on both sides of the Atlantic include pyramid building, sun worship, marriage between brothers and sisters in royal families, mummification, mummy masks, the wearing of false beards among priest kings, trepanning, script, calendar systems, the use of the mathematical zero, irrigation and terraced agriculture, cotton cultivation, spinning and weaving, special types of pottery, fitted megalithic masonry, the sling, the flat female figurine as house idol, birdmen deities, specialized musical wind instruments, reed boats, fish hooks, necropolises, mural painting and relief carving, adobe brick manufacture,

cylindrical and flat ceramic stamps and wheeled toys. All these have been discovered by scientists in restricted areas on both sides of the Atlantic: the oldest Mediterranean civilizations and Mexico-Peru. But considered one by one they are all elements and cultural traits that could have been thought of twice; they are inconclusive as evidence of transoceanic contact.

There is one case in particular that demonstrates how the same evidence can be ammunition for both diffusionist reasoning and isolationist. This is the Asian game of *parcheesi* which is very similar to the Mexican game of *patolli*. The diffusionist argues that because the two games are so similar, links between the two cultures must exist, and he proceeds to search for the links. The isolationist, conversely, argues that distance and other factors preclude the possibility of links and so the existence of the two games perfectly demonstrates that the human mind reacts inventively along parallel lines – however wide the distance between the two cultures that fostered the invention. The only way to resolve the dispute is to look at the oceans which, for one side are impenetrable, and for the other are so easily crossed.

Without question, an ocean is normally more effective than a desert, swamp, jungle or tundra in halting the geographic migration of aboriginal man. But an ocean, nevertheless, has pathways of currents and winds that directly facilitate its crossing; a brief study of these can shed popular doubts that the distances across water were too far, and would have taken too long, for ancient mariners. First, although Atlantic and Pacific currents do not apparently follow the most direct routes from one continent to another, for example the line of the equator, their sweeping curves are the same length as apparent straight lines. This is because the equator line, on a Mercator map projection, appears straight, whereas it is in fact a sweeping curve around the globe. The distance between two antipodal points is never shorter along the equator than along the great curves by way of the northern or southern hemispheres. Secondly, although the dead distance between two points can be measured in miles (and it often seems improbable that ancient man could have covered thousands of miles on a single voyage) this is not the same as the actual water surface covered. The speed of the current will itself carry a craft along with it, like a conveyor belt or an escalator. As an illustration, the dead distance between Peru and Tuamotu Islands in the Pacific ocean is 4,000 miles; yet the raft *Kon-Tiki* reached the islands from Peru after crossing only 1,000 miles of surface water. During that voyage the ocean itself was displaced 3,000 miles from east to west by the current. In order to return along the same route, a craft would have had to cover 7,000 miles of traveling surface water.

The oceans, rather than acting as barriers, are crossed by gigantic conveyor belts which transport anything that

U.S.S.R.

CHINA

INDIA

INDIAN OCEAN

Limit of drift ice

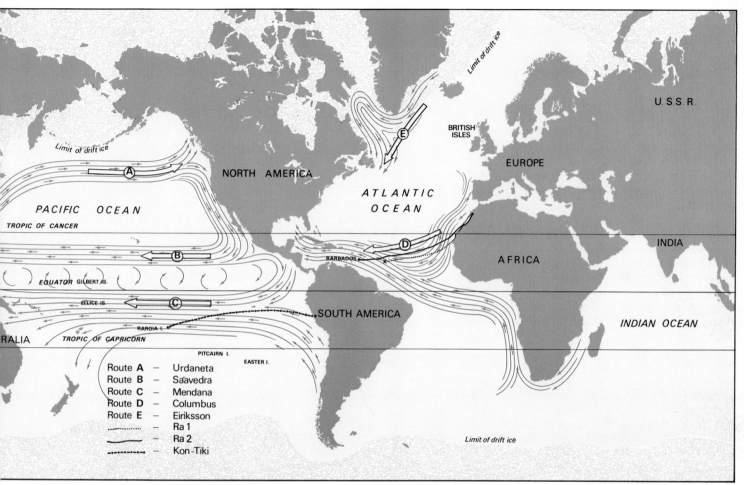

Route A – Urdaneta
Route B – Saavedra
Route C – Mendana
Route D – Columbus
Route E – Eiriksson
· · · · · · · – Ra 1
———— – Ra 2
-·-·-·-· – Kon-Tiki

stays afloat from one side to the other. Geographically speaking, the case for diffusion from A to B may be as logical and likely as it is meaningless and impossible from B to A. Once it is established that the geographical conveyor belt is favorable, then the case for diffusionism and trans-oceanic contact between peoples depends on the nature and chronology of the evidence for contact. And this evidence does exist. Pyramids, for example, are only found in Mesopotamia and Egypt on one side of the Atlantic, and in Mexico and Peru on the other. Mummi-fication has a similar limited occurrence on both sides of the Atlantic; and trepanation (the boring of holes in the skull) as well. All three *could* have evolved independently, but when they are found together, on either side of the Atlantic conveyor belt, then the likelihood of links be-tween their progenitors increases. Coincidence becomes a less tenable likelihood as other parallels are unearthed: the wearing of false beards among priest-kings, sun worship, reed boats, intermarriage among royal brothers and sisters. All *could* have evolved independently, but as the array of cultural parallels between the Old World and the New increases, so the likelihood of coincidence diminishes.

It is not merely the nature of the evidence that indi-cates cultural contacts, but also the time at which parallel artifacts and cultural traits appeared in the New World. Both schools of thought agree that the first peopling of America was by primitive hunter-gatherers who had little or no culture. The migrant from the Arctic tundra had neither agriculture, architecture, script, nor any other of the cultural achievements of the people subse-quently discovered by the Spanish in Mexico and Peru. And despite numerous archaeological digs and deep excavations in all the centers of high culture in Central and South America, no trace of gradual evolution from primitive society to civilization has been unearthed. Wherever archaeologists have dug, they have found that civilization appeared suddenly in full bloom, super-imposed upon a primitive, archaic society. The flourish of civilization begins at a peak and shows a gradual decline, rather than progress, through the centuries leading to the arrival of the first Europeans. The Spaniards were astonished at the Incas' high culture; yet the Inca borrowed much of their culture from earlier people, the Tiahuanaco and the Mochica, who had even more impressive civilization. Modern research has shown

9

that contact took place between these early pre-Inca civilizations and those contemporary in Mexico and Central America. There, the Aztecs, Toltec and Maya had drawn their basic lessons from the highly advanced civilization of the Olmec – a people who established Mexico's earliest civilization with script, calendar and pyramid building etc fully developed. They lived on the hot jungle coast of the Gulf of Mexico, unfavorable for the development of civilization, but located precisely where the marine conveyor from Africa ends.

Where, asks the diffusionist, is the evidence arguing independent cultural evolution in America? There is, as yet, none. On what basis, asks the diffusionist, can it be regarded that Peru and Mexico are too far from Europe and Africa for contact to have taken place? The isolationist can only reply that people of ancient Egypt and Mesopotamia were incapable of crossing the oceans; that they did not have the ships capable of staying afloat for such a length of time; that they did not have the knowledge of trans-oceanic voyages. But Columbus managed the voyage to America without navigational charts of the American waters. Pizarro crossed both the Atlantic and the jungle isthmus of Central America, and then sailed onwards in new ships, necessarily past the coastal swamplands, until he reached the favorable open terrain of Peru where he established a settlement. The Spanish knew nothing of the Americas; to Europeans of that time, the Atlantic was an ocean filled with dragons, and they thought it ended in a precipice at the horizon. Are we so blindfolded that we think that medieval Europeans could do what the truly great civilizations of Asia Minor and Egypt could not have done earlier?

Those organized people of antiquity had skills and knowledge that far surpassed anything imitated in the less spectacular cultures of Europe during the Middle Ages. The Egyptians, and their neighbors in Mesopotamia and Phoenicia, knew more about astronomy, the key to ocean navigation, than any Europeans contemporary with Columbus, Pizarro or Cortés. And the Phoenicians, in collaboration with the Egyptians, were circumnavigating Africa as early as the time of Pharoah Necho, two thousand years before Columbus ventured onto the high seas. We marvel at the abilities of the Ancients; their titanic pyramids and obelisks, their sophisticated mathematics, their amazing knowledge of rigging and the superb lines of their ships made from reeds and planks. And we marvel also at their spirit of exploration, now revealed in archaeological vestiges of their settlements – along the Atlantic coast of Morocco and beyond. We stand in awe of these achievements and the spread of their civilization. But was America too far for them to have gone?

One of the many parallels which the ancient civilizations of Mexico and Peru shared with Asia Minor and Egypt is the reed boat. It would seem fair to question the

seaworthiness of this craft; but in 1969 its capability was demonstrated when a Peruvian totora-reed boat sailed with an untrained crew the whole way from Peru to Panama. The voyage lasted two months. At about the same time, a papyrus-reed boat, built by central Africans according to the ancient Egyptian design, sailed from the African coast to the vicinity of Barbados. The following year, another papyrus-reed boat built by South American Indians crossed from Africa to tropical America in 57 days, covering a distance of more than 3,000 miles. The two Atlantic voyages proved, beyond reasonable doubt, the feasibility of a trans oceanic voyage by reed-boat. That the journey across the Panama isthmus could have been undertaken by ancient seafarers as easily as by Pizarro and his men goes without saying. Why should other people have acted differently if they preceded the Spaniards across the Atlantic and encountered precisely the same geographical conditions? To question this is to question one of the basic laws of isolationism – that people are apt to duplicate each other's feats. There is no reason to suppose that earlier Mediterranean voyagers would not have benefited from the same winds, currents and inclinations as the Spaniards.

There is more evidence than mere artifacts of New World civilization which leads us to postulate voyages across the Atlantic long before Columbus. This is in the field of ethnobotany, the study of cultivated plants. It is subject to far fewer variables, virtually none of which are available to human manipulation. In 1885 it was pointed out that the common garden bean was cultivated by the Greeks and Romans, and when it was discovered that the same bean was cultivated by aborigines of the New World, it was thought that it must have been introduced to America by the early Spaniards. But then the bean was discovered in a prehistoric cemetery at Ancon, on the coast of central Peru, where it had been buried as grave food. The burial long antedated the Spanish discovery of America, and when further discoveries of the bean were made in numerous other pre-Inca sites, the first explanation became completely untenable. It was now proposed by many that perhaps this bean had been unknown in the Old World until brought back from America by the Spaniards. Actually, however, it was a piece of botanical evidence pointing to early contact between the Old World and the New.

The bottle gourd represents another piece of similar evidence of early trans oceanic contact. This plant was widely cultivated in Africa long before Columbus and although of little food value, its rind was fire-dried and used as a watertight container throughout Mesopotamia, Egypt and Morocco. When the plant was discovered in the New World, where it was used for exactly the same purpose, botanists again thought it had been introduced by the Spaniards. Then bottle-gourds were unearthed in numerous pre-Columbian sites and a new theory was put forward to explain its presence. The gourds must have floated across the Atlantic from Africa, and the Indians had noticed that its rind made a useful container. But this attempt to wipe away an important African fingerprint in America could not stand closer inspection. Small edible objects, like gourds, would take four months to drift across the Atlantic. In that time they would be a certain prey for both sharks and hole-boring organisms such as shipworm. It was paradoxical that isolationists should propose that of two African culture elements – the gourd and the reed-boat – only the gourd could successfully drift across to America.

The cotton plant provided even more intriguing evidence. Wild cotton is short-linted, unspinnable and does not suggest any use to man. Yet, when Europeans arrived in America, they found the Indians throughout the high-culture area of Mexico and Peru wearing cotton clothes of high quality. Subsequent excavations in the mummy tombs of Peru revealed cotton cloths from the earliest pre-Inca period; cloths of such fineness and decorative pattern were unsurpassed anywhere. Apparently the founders of Peruvian civilization had come into possession of cultivated, long-linted cotton as well as the spindle-whorl and loom. Their methods were exactly those used in Egypt which themselves had come from Mesopotamia. But the real evidence only arrived after a study of cotton genetics revealed, through chromosome counts, that there are only three types of cotton plant in the world. All the cotton of the Old World, whether wild or cultivated, is of one group with 13 large chromosomes. In the New World however, there are two distinct groups; the wild American cotton has 13 small chromosomes, while the cultivated American cotton has a double set: 13 large and 13 small chromosomes combined. Since there was no large chromosome cotton among the wild American species, and the cultivated American variety was clearly a hybrid, some unaccounted species must have been available to early New World cotton cultivators. It would seem reasonable to suppose that they somehow obtained either the wild or the cultivated species from the Old World, both of which had the 16 large chromosomes absent in wild American cotton. There are, in fact, only two possible answers: either the 13 large chromosome species, typical of the Old World, happened to drift across the Atlantic just at the time civilization was developing in America, or it was brought intentionally at that time. But although cotton seeds may float undamaged, it seems improbable that on its arrival, Indians who had never seen a cotton field, much less a loom, would have known what to do with it.

If available evidence points to the strong possibility of pre-Spanish contact between the Old and New Worlds, only one question remains: why should Old World voyagers end up in the New World? And if they knew nothing of the existence of America, under what circumstances were the Atlantic voyages made? It is a long way from the eastern Mediterranean to the Gulf of Mexico, but at least 2,700 years before Columbus, Phoenicians were engaged in large scale exploration and colonization of the Atlantic coastlands. Although it is unlikely that marooned sailors, blown off course and shipwrecked, could have founded the high cultures of Mexico and Peru, the fact that Phoenicians were colonizing parts of Africa offers up another theory.

The transmission of concepts like hieroglyphic writing, pyramid building, mathematics and the techniques of mummification, required more than just a knowledge of their existence. Even a cursory knowledge of their working would not be enough for a teacher. A group of voyagers capable of founding a civilization like the Olmec must have been large enough to include representatives of the intellectual elite of its homeland; something like an organized group of colonizers, off course. Both archaeology and written history witness how large groups of colonists left the Mediterranean to found major settlements and trading posts along the coast of West Africa. In 450 BC, the Phoenician king, Hanno, sailed with 60 ships crowded with men and women to establish colonies—and Hanno was not a pioneer. Other organized expeditions, with roots in distant Phoenicia, had long before founded the large megalithic city of Lixus, far south of Gibraltar in today's Morocco just where the ocean current sweeps past directly towards the Gulf of Mexico.

The history of Lixus has vanished into the dawn of history. It was built by unknown sun-worshippers who orientated the gigantic megalithic walls according to the sun. Whoever founded and built Lixus, it is clear that astronomers, masons, scribes and expert potters were among them. And around 1000 BC just before Olmec civilization suddenly appeared in America, such colonizing voyages were common. Here, perhaps, we may find the link, the inspiration of the civilizations of the Americas. Aztec, Maya and Inca cultures all owed their origins to obscure local predecessors; in Mexico, civilization suddenly began with the Olmec who lived exactly at the other end of the ocean conveyor belt which sweeps everything that floats to the Gulf of Mexico.

Peoples of the Pacific islands

The great Oceanic culture of the Pacific embraces three peoples and their groups of islands: the Polynesians, the Micronesians and the Melanesians. They are culturally, racially and geographically distinct, but have at the same time some common features. This volume covering Oceania excludes the Melanesian islands (which are covered in Volume I of this series), except for the Fiji islands, which form a bridge between the western and eastern cultures of the south Pacific.

The geographical distinctions are the most obvious: the Micronesian islands are almost all north of the equator. Most of them, as the name Micronesia suggests, are small; they are of coral atoll formation, and include the Caroline, Mariana, Marshall and Gilbert islands. The Polynesian islands cover a much greater area than either of the other two main Pacific groups. They stretch from the partly Polynesian Ellice and Fiji islands in the west, as far east as the lonely Marquesa, Pitcairn and Easter islands; they reach south to New Zealand, and north to the Hawaiian group.

Evidence of the origins of the Oceanic peoples is scanty. The Micronesians are physically heterogeneous, and tend to be much smaller than the Polynesians, who are often massive, and of two physical types. Some Polynesians have relatively light skin and almost caucasian features; others, for example in Tahiti, are darker-skinned and mongoloid in appearance, often with the epicanthic fold of the eyelid. There is not enough evidence, however, confidently to trace any of these racial types to some Asiatic or American 'proto-Oceanic' race, or even to claim that the different physical types result from successive migrations. It is equally difficult to trace the origins of Oceanic languages. Micronesians and Polynesians both speak languages that are clearly Austronesian. But not enough is known about them to connect them with the Austronesian languages of Indonesia and mainland south-east Asia. There is still much research to do in Oceanic physical anthropology and linguistics.

Micronesia and most of Polynesia lie within the tropics, though some parts of Polynesia are sub-tropical. The high islands of volcanic origin have more rainfall than the low coral islands, and are more densely vegetated and fertile. But both Polynesian and Micronesian islands produce very few vegetables (mainly root vegetables like breadfruit, fern-roots, yams and taro), and almost no game. So the islanders depend on the sea for food. The crafts and customs of fishing are highly developed. Certain groups have rights to defined fishing grounds. Building canoes, navigational skills, making nets, fish hooks and other tools, and the magic and myth of the sea have deep roots in the culture and thought of the Pacific peoples. The customs of the sea have parallels ashore. For example land tenure systems mirror rights to fishing areas.

There are no metallic minerals: Captain Cook's iron nails fascinated Tahitians more than anything else. In the absence of wood, fibers and the uneatable parts of certain vegetables are the raw materials for domestic and artistic produce and manufacture. There is a vast range of tools and objects of art throughout Oceania: Fijians make pottery, and all islanders have developed elaborate religious and domestic architecture, basketry and bark cloth (tapa) work. They have many musical instruments, all kinds of hand weapons and a great variety of personal ornaments.

Polynesians and Micronesians both use the drugs kava and betel, though in different ways. Kava is a preparation made from roots of the *piper methysticum* pepper plant, and is drunk throughout Polynesia except in New Zealand and Easter Island; it is only found in one part of the Caroline Islands in Micronesia, where it is differently prepared. Melanesians chew betel for its slightly narcotic red juice, but in our area only the Pelew islanders chew it, and the inhabitants of Yap in the Carolines.

Pacific islands have differing social structures, which have all been more or less disrupted by western influences. The incestuous marriages of the Hawaiian aristocracy, the many-husbanded women of the Marquesas, and many-wived rich chiefs have almost completely disappeared. Even so all island society is still strongly hierarchical, and high positions are inherited. Often, as in Tonga, status comes from the mother and from her line. Christianity has partly undermined traditional hierarchies, but all Pacific peoples care passionately about family trees. Some inherited functions, like priestly duties in Hawaii, or bardic duties in the Marquesas and New Zealand, have been lost. But families still pass on precedence, land rights and an idea of tribal unity. In Tonga a vigorous royal lineage remains; in Fiji the chiefs have entered modern politics. These processes of change are described in several essays in this volume.

Polynesian social structures are founded on two concepts – *mana* and *tapu*. Micronesian social thought includes these concepts too, but much less centrally. *Mana* is an essence of power, a mystical force pervading nature, which tends to be concentrated in certain objects or people. In a man or woman *mana* would appear as luck, courage, wisdom, success in battle or in fishing, or in high social status. A high chief would be more likely to have it, but a commoner could show *mana* in brave deeds or exceptional qualities. *Tapu* (taboo) roughly means prohibition. A person or object which is *tapu* is set apart because it has become possessed by a supernatural power. The person of a high chief may be *tapu* and in turn can make objects, places or actions *tapu*. Commoners may make an object like a fruit tree or taro patch *tapu* to protect it from thieves. Violating *tapu* leads to supernatural retribution. *Mana* and *tapu* are clearly closely related, and strength in one relates to strength in the other. Almost any object touched or used by a high chief could become *tapu*, and could not be used until the *tapu*

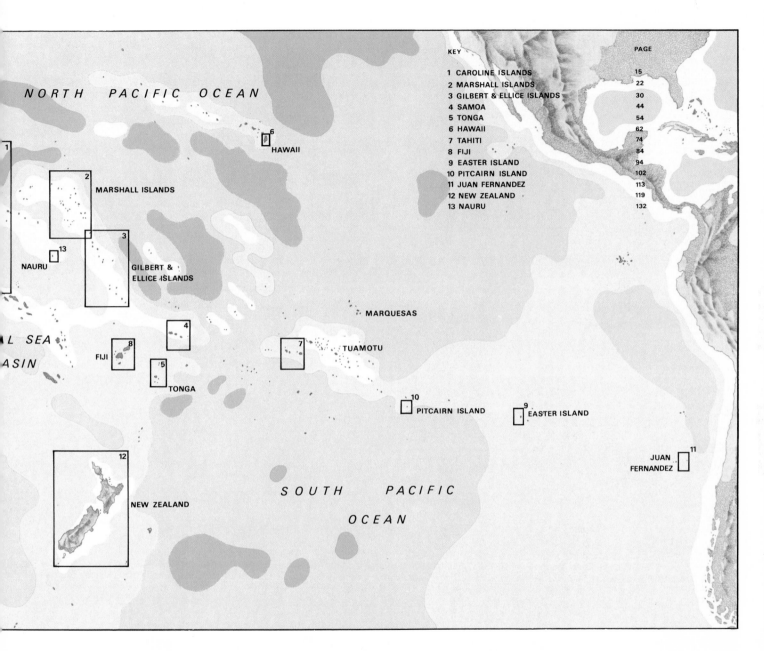

NORTH PACIFIC OCEAN

HAWAII

MARSHALL ISLANDS

NAURU

GILBERT &
ELLICE ISLANDS

MARQUESAS

TUAMOTU

FIJI

TONGA

PITCAIRN ISLAND

EASTER ISLAND

JUAN
FERNANDEZ

NEW ZEALAND

SOUTH PACIFIC

OCEAN

was released by a priest. Someone who unknowingly violated a *tapu* might be purified by certain ritual proceedings, but often the terrible consequences are believed to follow regardless of motive.

Oceania has changed greatly, and is still changing. The 'fatal impact' of Captain Cook's arrival and subsequent European traffic has altered or destroyed much of the native culture of the Pacific. Two world wars, ever-increasing communication, traders and tourists, the attitude of colonial powers to the Pacific peoples, and pressures towards integration have all had a profound effect. The Pacific islands have a culture; its disappearance will be a loss both to eastern and western worlds.

The Micronesian and Polynesian islands, strung out on either side of the equator, are the cultural bridge between east and west across the Pacific.

13

Caroline islanders
Micronesia

On Ushti atoll one of more than 500 Caroline Islands, islanders launch into 'The Church's One Foundation' with an American missionary.

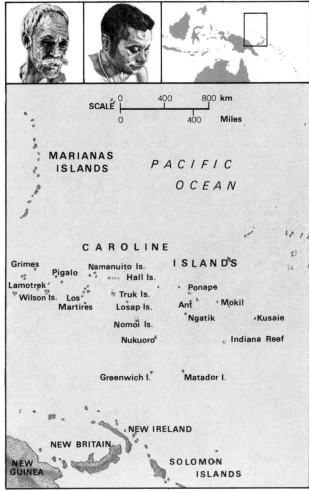

The green island is edged in white and surrounded by the deep blue of the ocean. It seems alone, adrift like the peak of a mountain that has broken through the clouds; then, as one draws closer, the green becomes diffused into the trees of a tropical forest, and breakers curl over a reef that shelters the shore. Beneath the tall palms whose trunks are like bare stalks, canoe houses with long, sloping thatched roofs huddle by the sharp white shore. Sometimes a small canoe with one or two people aboard breaks out and is paddled across the crescent-shaped lagoon. Occasionally a sailing canoe is stirred by the breeze and heads out to sea; but it is soon lost. Only its white sail is visible above the rolling waves.

Sailing east to west, for more than 2,000 miles, there are more than 500 islands like this. Just north of the equator, the Caroline Islands stretch across 400,000 square miles of ocean in a long archipelago. They are tiny dots in the Pacific, no larger than stars in a night sky. Some are volcanic and reach upwards two or three thousand feet with sharp ridges and deep valleys where thick vegetation covers everything but the rocky faces and the 15

high cliffs. Other islands are no more than sandy obtrusions above a thin coral reef. These coral atolls are formed by the gradual sinking of a former volcanic island, accompanied by a continuous upward growth of coral around it. The island of Ponape in the eastern Carolines is undergoing this process: as it has subsided the sea has drowned the lower parts of river valleys; the reef is separated from the main island by a deep lagoon. Shoals further to the south-east illustrate the final stages where atolls finally disappear beneath the waves.

Ethnically all the Caroline people are Micronesian, but across the archipelago, they may be separated into five groups, each speaking a distinct language and living in very different ways. Some are fishermen whose canoes cross hundreds of miles of sea in search of fish; others are farmers whose crops include tropical fruits like bread-fruit, coconut and bananas; they grow taro, yams and sugar cane, crops like maize, green onions and cucumber, and then there are the exotic fruits like limes and water-melons, oranges and pineapples.

The total land area of the Carolines is no more than 850 square miles, and of this the larger part is taken up by Palau and Yap in the west, Truk in the center, and

16

Ponape and Kusaie in the east. These, however, are not individual islands but groups of islands around which there are many more lesser islets and atolls. Each of the five has its own distinct language and its own culture; even within the groups there may be wide differences in dialect. In the Ponape group, for example, there are both high volcanic and low coral islands and the people from high islands – which for centuries have served as trade centers – rarely bother to learn the dialects of people from elsewhere. The languages may all share common origins, just as the people are all Micronesian, but they are now mutually unintelligible. The vast ocean not only facilitates travel, it also separates and isolates the groups of people.

In the west of the Caroline island group lies Yap, perhaps the most famous of the Caroline Islands. Early travelers to the Pacific called Yap the Venice of the Pacific, for the four main islands are separated by narrow channels and all are entirely surrounded by a shallow, green lagoon. Beyond there is a great reef which, in places, is two miles wide. These volcanic islands are rugged, broken and covered with forests of coconut and arica palms, bamboos and crotons – the source of the purgative, croton oil. The Yapese have developed a remarkable stone currency, in active use today alongside the currencies imported by the colonial powers. The stone coins vary from a few inches in diameter to ten or twelve feet. The larger stone coins weigh as much as five tons. A four-inch stone might purchase a fat pig, but a five-foot stone might, on the proper occasion, buy a whole village. Throughout Yap the name, ownership and history of every large stone is widely known.

Long ago the Yapese were masters of a loosely strung empire that extended far into the eastern Carolines. There was great trading activity and other islands were bound to pay tribute annually to appease Yap magicians who otherwise, it was thought, would cause famine, disease and storms. The Yapese remain a proud race and until the European intervention in the Pacific they were skilled artisans and cultural leaders. Woven cloth, dyes

Not all the Caroline islanders are Micronesian. These Kapangamarangi sailing canoes are from the Polynesian village of Poraklet.

and earthenware came from Yap; and their architecture and canoes were the most advanced in the Carolines. It was on Yap that the oldest customs prevailed; from there the arts of navigation were passed on to others. More than any other of the Caroline people, the Yapese preserve their traditional way of life. The design of their canoes has not changed for many generations.

A further four hundred miles east of Truk are the Ponape group of Islands. There, on one large volcanic island whose peak rises 2,500 feet above the sea and on the 23 smaller islands which ring it, great stone ruins of houses, forts, tombs and ceremonial places. Archaeological investigations are hampered by Ponapean superstition and sentiment; many feel that the remains of their forbears should not be disturbed and they refuse to approach the sites. Other Ponapeans feel that these taboos are pagan superstitions and demonstrate their Christian zeal by building pigsties out of the ancient structures, tombs or sacred enclosures. In 1907, one of the administrators of the eastern Carolines, Governor Berg, died suddenly on Ponape – according to native tradition it was shortly after he had tampered with the tombs of ancient kings at the Nan Matol ruins. Before his death, said the islanders, he had been pursued by the ghostly sound of shell-trumpets from the mountains.

These ruins testify to an earlier, unified rule on the islands by powerful chiefs or kings. The stonework seems likely to have been constructed well after the islands had first been settled when, as the islands provided well for their inhabitants, the population had increased and a social hierarchy and government had developed. These flourishing inhabitants were essentially the same people who populated the other islands of the group at around 1500 BC. They were people who had come from further west; some came from the Melanesian islands to the south; and later others came from Polynesia in the east. Ponape also has a rich body of semi-historical legends. According to Ponapean tradition, the islands were built under the guidance of two immigrant magicians, Sihpa and Sohpa. They built the site of the capital of the petty state of Deleur which eventually conquered all Ponape.

There were several sightings of the eastern Caroline islands by European ships during the 16th century. But apart from slight contact – probably to the islanders' amazement – the 17th and 18th centuries came and went and the islands were throughout completely ignored by passing ships. In 1828 a Russian ship finally came upon Ponape, thinking they had discovered it. The Captain recorded that it was the largest and the highest of the Carolines. Large canoes, which carried fourteen men, and small ones which carried only two, came out to meet him. He wrote of the islanders: 'Their wild visages full of mistrust, the great blood-filled eyes, the savagery and the wildness of these island dwellers made on us a right unpleasant impression . . .'

18

Taro is a staple food for most islanders and it has other uses too: this boy's umbrella is made of taro leaves.

Above the coral bed of the
sea off Ponape, rich in
marine life, an islander
spears a fish for his
family's evening meal.

19

The Ponapeans in the canoes danced and sang and gesticulated with their heads and their hands. One man tried to steal the sextant, but finally swam back to his canoe. Later, in the harbor, the Russians were again surrounded by canoes and noticed that in one there was a woman and that in all the canoes the natives had spears and slings which they tried to conceal under mats. During the visit an Irish sailor was already stranded on Ponape (though he made no contact with the Russians). He had been brought to a canoe house and accepted as a guest; to the delight of the islanders he had danced, an entertainment which was no doubt responsible for his safety. The islanders laid on a feast to welcome him. They roasted dogs and served kava, a mild narcotic drink, in his honor. Then they took him in a canoe to an empty hut where women tatooed him. He was treated well throughout his stay.

The years that followed brought ever-increasing contact with Europeans. Missionaries, whalers and naval ships all visited the islands. During World War II, the eastern Carolines were important Japanese bases and there was much destruction by American bombers. Towards the end of the war Ponape was a center of resistance by the islanders; yet perhaps a more common reaction to the troubles of war was a reversion to certain aspects of the old pagan religion. The islanders did not abandon Christianity outright, but many of them went into trances and came back with alleged visions or possession by spirits of the dead. Only when the war was finally over did these activities sink into obscurity.

Since the war the effect of contact between the islands and so different a form of civilization has been curiously undramatic. In each of the five petty states of Ponape there are two lines of chiefs who retain many of their chiefly functions. Their selection for the post is based both on a man's inherited rank and on his abilities. Though once a chief was not allowed to mix with the people, and at feasts he sat concealed in a special room, today the taboos on his person have relaxed. Kinship among most Ponapeans is a simple matter of recognizing every male relative of the father's generation – including his brothers, his wife's sisters' husbands and his male cousins – as a father; but grandfathers are also called fathers.

Among the island peoples, families and groups of relatives privately owned both cultivated and uncultivated land, fishing rights and houses. Land ownership was stable and secure and to the advantage of every member of the entire extended family. Inheritance was made not to the individual, but to the family or group. It provided for both old and young, and protected the welfare of all who could not actively cultivate crops or go out fishing. The result of emphasis on a new system of individual property ownership has been a weakening of family ties.

Ponape has a large land area and has remained a largely agricultural community. The islanders have

Festively dressed in a skirt of dyed grasses a Ponapean girl dances squatting down, beating time with a stick against a board on her lap.

The tombs of the ancient kings lie in the ruins of Nan Maton on Ponape testifying to an earlier, more centralized, rule.

cultivated their land ever since they first inhabited them – although the number of different plants was never very great and even now few European crops have been adopted on a large scale. The Ponapeans cultivate pandanus around the villages on all the islands, so that they can build huts, canoe houses and ceremonial houses and make mats of the pandanus leaves. Coconuts are not only important to the islanders as a source of food and drink, but also for the husks with which they make cord used in the construction of both canoes and houses. Ponapean men wear the fibers from new unfolded fronds as 'grass' skirts on ceremonial occasions.

The Ponapeans' large out-rigger canoes are capable of sailing far out into the ocean. They use smaller canoes, with shallow drafts, for lagoon fishing and transport and despite the recent introduction of outboard motors, the sails and paddles are still the primary means of motion. The islanders use both nets and hooks and lines to catch the fish when at sea; inshore from reefs, they catch fish in baskets which they lower into the water; around the reef they gather in the fish in a seine net supported by poles; they also impale fish on spears with two or three points. On low islands almost every man knows how to fish, but not every man however can build a canoe. This is an art left to the master canoe builders who know the correct proportions and are always called in to give the hull its correct shape. They work only with hand tools, digging out from the trunk of a tree, shaping and molding the hull, until its lines are smooth and straight.

When all is done and fish are cooking over the fire, and breadfruit and bananas have been pounded into a *poi*, and the kava is ready, the Ponapeans tell their traditional tales, dance and sing old songs to the sound of guitars or harmonicas brought by the Europeans – for their native instruments, the drum and the nose flute have long been forgotten. Men sometimes have standing dances with decorated dance paddles which they flash and turn. Women have sitting dances, with small sticks which they strike together or against a board resting on their laps. Occasionally the men use long staffs and leap about, striking the poles together in fixed patterns; these dances are considered good training for a man or boy. But most Ponapean dances are loose and relaxed, and precisely controlled in their movements. On Ponape, people have given their own twist to tales found widely in the Pacific Islands. A common tale is one of a man who chops down a tree to make a canoe, but each morning he finds the tree standing again in full foliage. He is only able to finish his canoe when he has made the appropriate offering to the nature spirit. On Ponape this tale has a special ending – the cause of the man's trouble is his failure to apologise for his poor work to an insignificant looking passer-by who is really a super-natural being. The Ponapeans believe in speaking modestly.

21

Marshall islanders
Micronesia

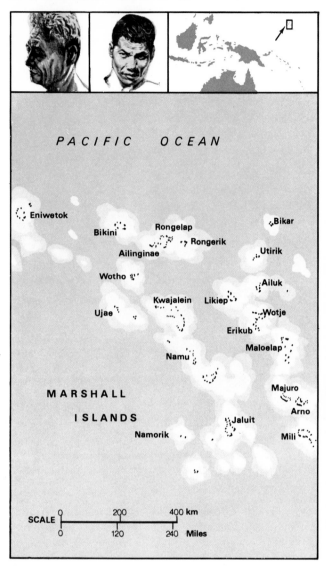

PACIFIC OCEAN

Eniwetok
Bikini
Rongelap
Bikar
Rongerik
Ailinginae
Utirik
Wotho
Ailuk
Kwajalein Likiep
Ujae
Wotje
Erikub
Maloelap
Namu

MARSHALL

ISLANDS
Majuro
Arno
Jaluit
Namorik
Mili

SCALE 0   200   400 km
       0   120   240 Miles

he countless islands of the Pacific Ocean, with their different geographical and political groupings and their curious names, are blurred and confused in many people's minds. They can indeed be hard to distinguish and remember. But among the Marshall Islands, there is one atoll whose name has become a household word, everywhere and unforgettably – Bikini.

After World War II, before the Test Ban Treaty was signed, certain great powers were preoccupied with the testing of nuclear weapons. The Russians could use their wide open spaces for this purpose. The British used Christmas Island, one of the islands of their Gilbert and Ellice colony. And in 1946, in the same way, the Americans approached the 166 inhabitants of Bikini Atoll, and told them through their chief Judal that their homeland was about to be engulfed by an unimaginable fireball, and

23

On Bikini, most famous of
the Marshalls, Americans test
the level of radiation years
after the 1946 atomic blast.
It is now at safety level.

Marshall islanders Micronesia

All life on the island
and in the sea around was
destroyed by the fall-out.
These fish were affected
by radioactivity.

24

The first people to return to
Bikini were American
technicians, to assess the
damage the bomb had caused
this doomed Pacific island.

that they would do well to move.

Bikini and the other Marshall Islands lie within the United States Trust Territory of the Pacific, and the islanders were not in a position to argue. Like all Micronesians, they were deeply attached to their island home; and they were particularly reluctant to leave the spirits of their dead, who would still linger around the old home and could not be transplanted. But they agreed to be moved: to Rongerik Atoll at first, 109 miles to the south-east, and then to Kwajalein, and finally to Kili Island at the southern extremity of the Marshalls.

Bikini and Eniwetok are two of the Marshall Islands, so named after the English sea captain who partially explored them in 1788. They form the easternmost group within Micronesia – an area which also includes the Carolines, the Marianas, and the Gilbert and Ellice Islands. The Marshalls, lying wholly within the northern hemisphere, are stretched out in two long parallel chains, running north-north-west to the south-south-east. There are 34 of them altogether: 14 atolls and two islands in the Ratak chain which lies to the east, and 15 atolls and three islands in the Ralik chain to the west – those words meaning towards dawn and towards sunset.

The Marshall Islands are, without exception, low. The highest, Likiep, rises only 34 feet above high water level, and this is really exceptional: most rise only five or six feet. Each atoll consists of a number of long thin islands of coral formation, lying in a roughly circular or oval pattern to enclose a central lagoon. They are particularly narrow: the widest island in the whole archipelago, Wotje, is less than a mile across, and most can be crossed in a few minutes' walk. The Marshallese live, therefore, not only at sea level but on the sea's edge, making their homes on thin ribbons of land, with the huge openness of sea and sky always around them.

They came at an unknown date originally from south-east Asia to these scattered, sandy islands. Like other Micronesians they are of mixed negroid and mongoloid stock, but they are lighter-skinned and more Polynesian in their features than the Kanakas of the western Carolines and Micronesians who live closer to Asia. The Marshalls were not an ideal place to settle, but they did provide a home, and were able to support a small population by careful horticulture and by intensive fishing. Furthermore they were free from malaria which is endemic in nearly all Melanesia. Their scant resources turned out to be a positive advantage: since their islands offered little temptation to overcrowded peoples from other islands and the Asian mainland, the Marshallese were left in relative peace.

These atolls are frequently swept by storms and typhoons. There is practically no topsoil, rainfall is low, there are no springs or rivers, and water is scarce. Breadfruit, bananas and other vegetables are practically unobtainable. The islanders have started to cultivate arrowroot with some success, and consider it a great

delicacy when grated and fried in coconut oil; but their economy has always depended largely on the sea and the coconut palm.

The coconut tree meant wealth, and the affluence of each island or village depended on how many trees it had to provide food and drink, cloth and cordage, wood and building materials. Their coconuts were both smaller and scarcer than elsewhere in Micronesia, and the various products of that useful tree would not be used lightly when a substitute was available. Bone and stone were scarce too, and the sea provided substitutes. The giant clam provided the most usual cutting implements, fish hooks were of turtle shell; spears were shell-tipped. And where a Polynesian would use coconut fiber – for example, to tie the shell blade of his knife to its wooden handle – the Marshallese would often use strips of shark skin. The sea is also a rich source of food: the reefs provide squid, crabs and shellfish, bonito and other big fish come from the open sea, while small fish are caught in the lagoons. Like most Pacific peoples the Marshallese were great sea voyagers and traders. Their canoes were plank-built, lashed with coconut fiber and caulked with gum, and sometimes fitted with outrigger or sails or both.

And so, living in their rectangular and palm leaf thatched houses, the Marshallese enjoyed a simple but sufficient subsistence economy. Clothing was simple: everyone was naked above the waist, the men wore loincloths and the women wore skirts of bark or pandanus leaves while the children went completely naked. Tattooing was very popular: high-ranking professionals, using all bone blades, made patterns which indicated social rank.

Marshallese society was, by tradition, stratified: status comes from membership in high-ranking kinship groups rather than from individual achievements, though it could be improved by warfare, and the chiefs wielded absolute authority.

The Marshallese are a gentle, courteous people. The qualities that they value most highly in a man are kindness, generosity, and a low voice: no insult would wound them more deeply than an accusation of meanness. 'Love to you!' is their traditional greeting. Flowergarlands, fans, mats, or other small gifts traditionally change hands when strangers meet.

The impact and influence of the white man upon their society was slow and uneven. The islands offered no obvious incentive for exploration or colonization. Various Spanish expeditions visited them in the 16th century. Captain Marshall came in 1788. Russians came to explore and make maps between 1803 and 1823. Some sixty years later they were recognized as a Spanish possession. After the Spanish-American War they were sold to Germany. In 1914 they were seized and developed and colonized extensively by the Japanese. During World War II they were painfully captured by the Americans and were put under a United Nations Trusteeship in 1947. Today they are moving towards self-government.

With political changes the old pattern of Micronesian life was gradually disrupted. The intruders' motives were more commercial than imperialistic, though missionaries came too. The Protestant 'Boston Mission' established itself on Hawaii in 1820, and moved on from there to many other islands, including the Marshalls. One consequence of this was that the islanders – impressed by the obviously greater power of the white man's God – became slightly ashamed and secretive about their own religious tradition, and came in due course to forget it, so that little is now known about its exact pattern. But the missionaries at least made it possible for the Marshallese to believe that some white men were good and could be trusted. The traders had tended to give an opposite impression, especially the whalers of the 19th century, who came from Nantucket, Sydney and elsewhere to inflict their rum, their diseases and their lechery upon the islands.

In 1885 for the Germans who established a protectorate, the Marshalls were only interesting as a source of copra and shells. They stopped the chiefs from feuding and inflicting capital punishment, but otherwise they left 25

Marshall islanders Micronesia

Bikinians longed for return to their homeland all through their long exile, but when a few did return they found it barren and lifeless.

(Center) King Judal of Bikini hoped to return to his island but he died of cancer on Kili just before the return began.

the islanders alone. When the Japanese took the islands over, by a decision of the Peace Conference after World War I, they had more positive ideas. They felt that the Marshalls, the Carolines and the Marianas could well be colonized as an outlet for Japan's crowded population – a source of wealth as well, and a springboard for potential conquests in the future. But in fact the limited resources of the Marshalls meant that the Japanese impact – like the German impact before it – was weaker there than it was elsewhere in Micronesia. To some extent the authority of the chiefs was undermined. The Germans

26

The 1946 atom bomb caused 10 million tons of the Pacific to explode into a mushroom half a mile wide. It was an experiment in military defense.

had allowed them to farm the taxes, which were collected in the form of copra. Their authority, otherwise weakened by the presence of an overriding foreign power, was in this limited way reinforced. But under the Japanese the chiefs were by-passed, and copra was sold direct to the traders and the tax levied upon it directly. The chiefs got their share but lost their dominant position. Thus the Japanese were partly responsible, in an indirect way, for the end of the old stratified society of the Marshalls and the development of the present situation, in which chiefs and nobles and commoners dress and live alike and have equal votes in the islands' affairs. But in general, under both foreign regimes, only a few traders and officials came to the islands. For the most part the people were left to their subsistence economy, their fishing and cultivation of copra.

Like many other islands in the Pacific, the Marshalls suffered heavily in World War II. Its effects and after-effects divorced them more surely than anything else from their traditional past. When the Americans captured Kwajalein, in 1944, there was nothing living there but seven coconut trees. Later on this atoll – one of the world's largest – became the center and base for enormous naval and air forces.

When that war ended the Americans made generous efforts to heal war-time scars. The Marshallese were fed and clothed. They were given injections, which some of them erroneously supposed would guard them against misfortune, and were purged of the venereal diseases which the early white civilizers had conferred upon them. The Americans also built and replaced schools and hospitals. Coconuts and pandanus were replanted. They gently reduced the authority of the chiefs and nobles still further, and democratic institutions started to develop. An over-riding benevolence supervised all things, prices in particular.

The sea remains a lavish source of food, but the importance of copra has declined, and the economy of the islands is definitely precarious. Micronesians have always been a creative people, and they now sell the mats, baskets and wood-carvings which they once made for their own daily use as souvenirs or curios. But the people have now acquired tastes and habits which cannot easily be supported on these rather limited economic bases. In the old days expectations were simple but could be realized, and the Marshallese were 'free' in most senses of that rather complicated word. Now they have started to live like Americans, in some of the islands at least, on however modest a scale, and they have needs which they never knew before: bicycles, refrigerators, flour, rice, tinned foods, sugar, tea, coffee, western clothing.

They are also great cinema-goers, having recovered from their original shock and embarrassment at Hollywood's love scenes. But all these things have to be paid for, and the coconut palm is no longer quite the symbol of wealth that it once was – especially since, after

Life returned slowly to Bikini
in the form of tough grasses
and scrub, but all that was
beautiful and graceful
in nature had gone.

Marshall islanders Micronesia

In rectangular palm-leaf
huts Bikinians have made a
home on Kili, where they
depend on the sea and coconut
palms for their livelihood.

Bikinians discuss their
return with US officials.
The difficulty was to be in
getting a living from
the tortured land.

The Marshallese have their own 'Christian Church of the Marshall Islands,' firmly rooted in a devout New England form of protestantism.

the nuclear mishaps of 1954, some Japanese purchasers have made things harder by requiring the copra they purchase to be certified free of radio-activity.

The economic future of these islands is therefore something of a problem; especially since – here as elsewhere in the Pacific – a great spaciousness paradoxically surrounds an overcrowded and overpopulated people. The Marshall Islands occupy a part of the earth's surface which is eight times the size of New York State. But it is nearly all sea: the actual land area amounts to only about 61 square miles, or less than a quarter of the area of New York City. This limited space has to accommodate and support a population which rose from 10,553 in 1948 to 17,363 in 1963, and is still rising.

Planned emigration may perhaps reduce over-crowding, as in the Gilbert and Ellice Islands, and the development of a canned fish industry for export may help to balance the Marshall Islands' accounts. The sea, certainly, is their greatest asset.

But it would be a mistake to exaggerate the distress of the islanders, or the disruption of their ancient and simple life. To some extent they are both urbanized and Americanized. The main town and port, and the administrative capital of the whole United States Trust Territory, is Majuro in the Ratak chain. (An earlier capital, Jaluit in the Ralik chain, was destroyed by 'Typhoon Ophelia' in 1958 when winds reached 135 knots, the whole island was flooded to a depth of several feet, all the houses and most of the coconut trees were swept away, and 16 people died.) But on the smaller atolls, away from Majuro and Kwajalein and urban pressures, something very like the old life still continues.

It is a hard life and a healthy one. The Marshallese have always been a hardy and vigorous people, and all the more so since they have had modern medical and public health services. Athletic contests between different villages are extremely popular, and so are canoe races. A racing canoe, perhaps 30 feet long and only 30 inches wide, can reach a speed of 20 miles an hour. Children like to race one crab against another, at a somewhat gentler pace.

And theirs is also a courteous, gentle, and honourable way of life, pious and strict as well. Most Marshallese now belong to the 'Christian Church of the Marshall Islands', an independent Church of their own, but one that is deeply rooted in the Protestant and Puritan tradition of New England. Drinking and smoking and swearing are frowned upon, and the Lord's Day is observed most reverently.

So it continues, in the spirit of that Protestant piety, the old subsistence life of fishing and coconut-gathering and copra-drying. On these outlying islands and atolls a stove or a refrigerator, a fresh-water tank or an outhouse lavatory mark its possessor as a man of substance. But by the standards of most of the world, many of the Marshallese are still free of the tyranny of possessions. 29

Gilbert and Ellice islanders
Micronesia

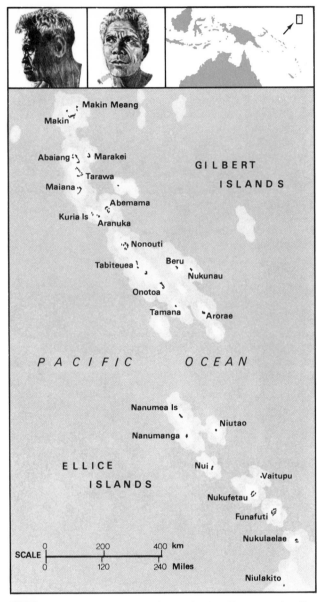

Makin Meang
Makin
Abaiang Marakei
Tarawa
Maiana
GILBERT
ISLANDS
Abemama
Kuria Is
Aranuka
Nonouti
Tabiteuea Beru
Nukunau
Onotoa
Tamana Arorae

PACIFIC OCEAN

Nanumea Is
Niutao
Nanumanga
ELLICE Nui
ISLANDS Vaitupu
Nukufetau
Funafuti
Nukulaelae

SCALE
0   200   400 km
0   120   240 Miles

Niulakito

The paradise of the Gilbert and Ellice peoples lies westwards across the sea in the land of Matang. Fairskinned gods and ancestors live there, eating *te rengu,* the half-remembered food that makes the teeth red, and Nakaa the Law Giver keeps the Gate. It was Nakaa who drove the early fathers out of the land of Matang, because they played with women under the women's sweet-scented tree of death, and they had to sail far away from the west. Nakaa sits at the gate of death, with a net and a row of stakes, and strangles every dead traveler to the lands of the west whose relations had not straightened his way with the ritual of *Te Kaetikawai.* Those who had committed incest, or dishonored their ancient ancestors' bones and shrines were impaled on the stakes. But sinless ghosts can pass to Bouru and

31

Missionaries have failed to
stamp out Gilbertese magic
and ritual: here an islander
tends the bones of a friendly
ancestral spirit, Chief Korabi.

Gilbert and Ellice islanders Micronesia

Most Ellice islanders own tame frigate birds. They fly away for a few days, but they always come back — for a good meal.

All Polynesians love dancing: children on remote Nanumanga wait in ceremonial painted home-dyed dress to dance in honor of a visiting official.

Collecting copra for export can be dangerous outside the reefs, when lagoons are too shallow: but the Gilbertese are highly skilled sailors.

32

Marira, Miwaiku and Neineaba beneath the western horizon, though they can never regain Matang. And Au, the god of the rising sun, who sprang from the Tree of Knowledge of Matang, protects the islanders and will come one day with his fair-skinned company from Matang.

Te renga, the food of the western ancestors, was very likely the drug betel, which stains the mouth red and is slightly intoxicating. It has never grown on the Gilbert and Ellice islands. Almost all islanders believe it was the diet of the fair or red-skinned gods of the race (like the spirit of the pandanus, Tabu-anki the Thunder-God, and Riiki the Eel whose belly is the Milky Way). An early race-memory of betel suggests a link between the Gilbert and Ellice chain and Indonesia, the center of betel-chewing. Standing at the gates of the Pacific, the Moluccan area of Indonesia seems the likely origin of the migrations that brought the Bouru-Matang-renga beliefs to the Gilberts. Also Bouru resembles Buru, the name of a large island in the Moluccan area. Matang is a widespread Indonesian place-name between Matang of Sarawak and Medang of New Guinea.

The correspondences support the theory that the betel-eaters and other migrants who peopled the Pacific came from Indonesia and traveled as far as Samoa. These seafarers were not the first inhabitants of Oceania: the first were a dark-skinned race of pygmies, from whom perhaps comes the Gilbertese god Na Areau Te Kikinto (the mischief-maker), a stinking black dwarf of frizzy hair and evil spells. The pygmies were followed by other dark-skinned, probably negroid and mongoloid people, and much later by sea-farers of two types: beautiful brown-skinned mongoloids from Asia and a tall fair people with red beards. One or other of these peoples developed the outrigger canoe from which the great Gilbertese tradition of navigation comes.

The islanders in the Gilbert and Ellice group were involved for hundreds of years in bloody and sporadic wars with each other, with Tongans and especially with Samoans. For generations blood feuds raged: women who went outside their villages could expect to be killed or raped; there was some cannibalism and, at the very least, victorious warriors bit their victims' eyeballs ceremoniously in two, a practice which lasted into the 20th century. It was only with the Pax Britannica of the white-skinned lady of Matang Kuini Kabitoria (Queen Victoria) that the islanders really felt secure.

They greeted the white men who arrived in the 18th and 19th centuries as the legendary men of Matang, claimed their relationship, and treated them with a proud brotherliness. Their affection for all Europeans explains their courteous peaceful treatment of them. And whatever harm the later English arrivals did, at least they brought peace and a reasonable administration; in 1915 they made the islands into a crown colony. There was one man of Matang in the first years of the

33

The sea surrounds the life of villages like Abiang. To catch an octopus, one islander lowers his partner — as bait — from the reefs where octopuses hide.

Gilbert and Ellice islanders Micronesia

Family life is intimate and free from painful conflict: here a Gilbertese mother puts her child to sleep by singing as it lies on her stomach.

Trips to lavatories are rather public as they are built out into the lagoon on stilts, so that the tide will remove the excrement.

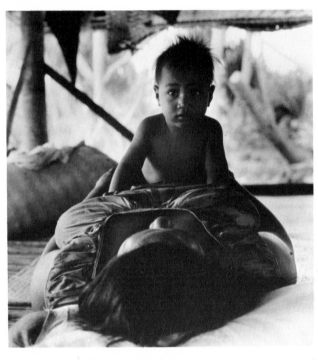

century who learnt their language and customs, and became a member of the Karongoa, the sun clan. He was tattooed with the mark of the serpent, the sun-god's spouse; he was a fair judge and a brave man and his name is famous throughout the islands: he was called Kurimbo – Sir Arthur Grimble.

He knew the Gilbertese before contact with foreigners had done them much harm. They were no longer war-like, but gentle, infinitely courteous and a people with great legends and poetry, and they and their islands were extraordinarily beautiful. The 16 Gilbert atolls and islands lie in an arc five hundred miles long that connects Micronesia with Polynesia. To the south-east are four islands and five atolls making up the Ellice Islands; to the east are the Phoenix Islands, Fanning and Christmas Island, and to the west is the fertile Ocean Island (Baanaba) which is rich in phosphate, and which rests on the back of a giant turtle at the bottom of the sea. Scattered over 2 million square miles of the western Pacific, the islands' area is only about 342 square miles.

The islands and atolls produce little except coconuts, pandanus and copra. Villages almost always lie on the calm leeward side. Above the beach in the shade of the palms are thatched cook-houses and canoe sheds, and the dwellings follow broad flower-lined roads parallel to the shore.

The islanders have different characteristics. The Ellice islanders are Polynesians, with some Samoan and Tongan blood. The language resembles Samoan. They are thought a very cheerful and exuberant people, despite their poverty and the attentions of the slave-traders in the past. The Gilbertese are Micronesian, physically smaller and their language is close to Melanesian. They are said to be more reserved than the Ellice islanders. But they have much in common. Almost all are now either Catholic or Protestant; there are very few pagans, except in the remote atolls. Each island has a clan system centering around a large village *maneaba* or speaking house where all public affairs are discussed. The Gilbertese love humor, rhetoric and litigation. Their ceremonious, circumlocutory language and courtesies, their soft voices and traditional responses make *maneaba* meetings both memorable and drawn-out. All islanders excel at dancing, which like most dance is originally religious. Formality, especially on the Gilberts, pervades social life. If a person crosses another's line of vision or conversation he must ask '*E Matauninga te aba?*' 'are the people offended?' For the Gilbertese say

Some of the fastest craft
in the world, Gilbertese
racing canoes can travel
at 20 knots across the
lagoons with a good wind.

35

Islanders build simple open
houses from coconut trees,
raising them on stilts to
keep out the rats and the
damp when the rains come.

Gilbert and Ellice islanders Micronesia

In the traditional *maneaba*
the young islanders' cosmology
is painstakingly displaced.
Yet old folklore customs and
dances cling on tenaciously.

Roman Catholics, who have
been closer to the Gilbertese
than other Christians, have
brought, if not tolerance,
western schools and medicine.

even of high-ranking people 'Small is the voice of a chief.' Even a chief must be courteous.

And despite a hundred years with Christian missionaries and the islanders' conversion to Christianity, pagan magic has not died in the minds of the Gilbertese. *Wawi* is killing magic and *bonobono* is good magic that averts *wawi*. This magic was of two kinds, *te kawai* (ritual) and *te tabunea* (incantation or spell). Magic and magical presences are part of everyday life: objects and names have spirits which can be governed by charms and spells. There is magic to protect coconuts, magic to sour a woman's oven and enrage her family, magic to obtain a woman or send her mad. A canoe must be protected from sharks and weather by incantations at its naming. A girl at the beginning of puberty is especially vulnerable to sterility spells and her hair and nails and urine must be guarded from theft. Magic can produce greater virility, or kill a disdainful girl with a fearful 'false' pregnancy by the evil swordfish spirit Terakunene. Grimble as a member of the Royal Karongoa (sun) clan learnt protective spells, which must have been useful when a witch doctor poisoned his coconut toddy with juice from the cantharides fly. He also learnt to bless his fish-hook with magic.

Though evil magic threatened every islander, there was a great deal of benign magic, and the spirits of the ancestors were benign too, and gave loving protection. They often returned to their skulls and bones, and the Gilbertese liked to show respect for their bones, oiling them, bathing them in the sea, speaking to them and very often sharing a pipe of tobacco with a much loved skull, since the departed ones could get no tobacco in the lands of the west. Shrines of bones were respected and in times of drought or danger the whole hamlet would bring offerings and ask for help. Christian missionaries, among other crimes, such as clothing the Gilbertese women in ugly Mother Hubbard shrouds, destroyed these ancestral shrines, often childishly and crudely in an hysterical and undignified way. This rooted out ancient loves but not ancient superstitions. Dishonoring ancestors and disrespect to their bones was a crime and a disgrace equalled only by incest. All the Gilbert and Ellice people believed that their *mauri* (safety, prosperity) depended on avoiding these two sins. Much as they honored the white man of Matang, this was hard to forgive, though many of them were already half-converted to Christianity when shrine-ragging first started. By the 1960s ancestral shrines and bone-tending had become rare.

Christian interference did have a disruptive effect on Gilbertese marriage and morals. According to the complex traditional kinship systems a man might share his wife on occasion with a brother *(eiriki)* or with an old relation *(tinaba)*. He might also have as secondary wives the uterine sisters of his first wife, often when they were plain or unlikely to get their own husbands. Everyone Grimble talked to found these arrangements satisfactory; they cemented the relationship between affection, responsibility for children and siblings, and (by reciprocal agreements) land ownership. But the British made polygamy and *tinaba* illegal at the turn of the century. Honorable women were suddenly adultresses, children became bastards, and there were many suicides.

Of all the Gilbertese traditions, according to Grimble, two are outstandingly impressive – their knowledge of the sea and their poetry. They are uncannily skilled navigators and can plot courses by the stars, or by the different smells of different waters. They avoid the treacherous currents and reefs almost by instinct, and have countless ways of catching fish. One of the oddest and rarest is their way with porpoises.

The *utu* (a blood-related group) of Kuma on Butaritari Island possessed the power of *Te Binekua* of calling porpoises. This family belongs to Mone, the land under the sea. The caller sleeps and his spirit goes to Bikaati and dives down into Mone, and entreats the porpoises to come ashore with him to dance. The porpoise king allows this, and the porpoises swim to the village. The caller wakes and the whole village goes in feasting clothes to the beach and welcomes the porpoises in the shallow waters, playing with them, talking to them and finally each brings a 'brother' ashore, only to slaughter him brutally. Though this defies western credulity, western men have witnessed it.

Less strange but equally dismaying is octopus catching. One man swims as live bait into the octopus' tentacles. Just as they enfold him and the gaping beak nuzzles him, his companion darts down and bites the octopus between the eyes, killing it at once. An octopus can tear all the skin off a man's arm with only one sucker, so the 'bait' must trust his companion perfectly.

The islanders delight in outwitting sharks too. Sometimes they taunt the shark, like a swimming matador, and slit its belly as it charges past: its genitals are very valuable in virility spells. Usually they just wrestle with enchanted fish hooks. The sea provides more than food. Coral and shells make cutting implements, the sting ray's tail used to make lethal arrow tips, and the little shell fish nimatanin is used as a barometer.

The peculiar force and vigor of Gilbertese songs, myths and incantations has survived time and translation. Even the names of children and canoes are beautiful – Movement of Clouds, Child of the Tide Race. The roots of poetry lie in magic, and the strength of Gilbertese myth and poetry is that it is close to its roots. The idea of Golden Age is itself a myth, but perhaps the Gilbert and Ellice islanders lived through something like one for a short time between World War I and World War II when a man of Matang lived with them, learning and writing down their poetry and trying to protect their ways. Now, though the islands have resisted westernization, they have the universal problem of overpopulation, and increasing material desires.

Europeans and the Pacific— the fatal impact

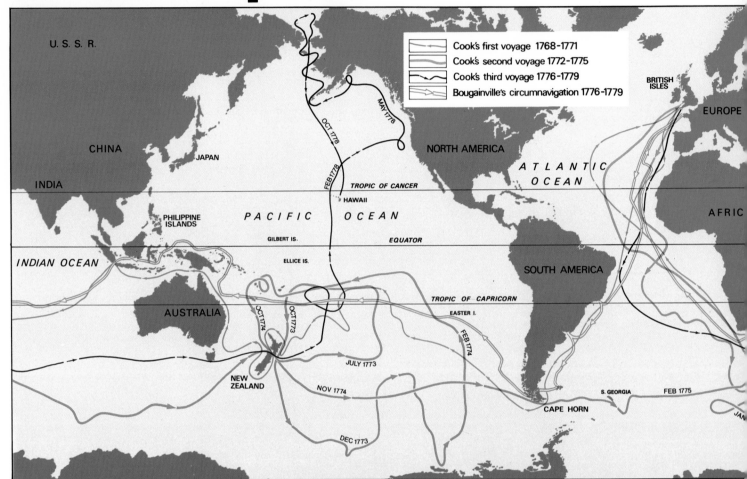

Legend:
- Cook's first voyage 1768-1771
- Cook's second voyage 1772-1775
- Cook's third voyage 1776-1779
- Bougainville's circumnavigation 1776-1779

U.S.S.R.

CHINA

JAPAN

INDIA

PHILIPPINE ISLANDS

INDIAN OCEAN

AUSTRALIA

NEW ZEALAND

PACIFIC OCEAN

GILBERT IS.

ELLICE IS.

HAWAII

TROPIC OF CANCER

EQUATOR

TROPIC OF CAPRICORN

EASTER I.

NORTH AMERICA

SOUTH AMERICA

ATLANTIC OCEAN

BRITISH ISLES

EUROPE

AFRICA

CAPE HORN

S. GEORGIA

OCT 1778

MAY 1778

FEB 1778

OCT 1774

OCT 1773

JULY 1773

NOV 1774

DEC 1773

FEB 1774

FEB 1775

First the Europeans decimated the population with their diseases. Now their medicine has led to a serious threat of overpopulation.

When Captain James Cook sailed his ship, the *Endeavour*, into Tahiti's Matavai Bay in 1769, it was the beginning of continuous contact between Europeans and the islands of the south and central Pacific. Three other European ships had in fact already visited the islands, but none of these had stayed more than five weeks. Cook's ship was to stay for three months and he and many of his men were to live ashore. Little by little the sailors and the islanders, eating the same food and caught up in the routine of long, enervating Tahitian days, came to know one another. The islanders proved to be incorrigible thieves and an uneasy quiet followed whenever a theft was discovered. Cook was strict. He always sought out the thief and soon the islanders grew to respect him. The Tahitians also proved to be far removed from the puritan ethics of English life. The sailors were captivated by the beauty, the apparent innocence – and the willingness – of the Tahitian girls, many of whom gave themselves freely to the Englishmen.

In the excitement of this first prolonged contact between the islanders and the Englishmen there was little hint of the disasters which were to follow. It was a honeymoon of a kind. Even Cook trusted himself to sleep in the Tahitians' huts at night, though he sometimes had cause to regret it because of the thieving. Yet even at this early stage the honeymoon had a certain unsavory side. There was soon venereal disease among the islanders – something they had never known before. In his journal, Cook noted somberly that venereal disease 'may in time spread itself over all the islands in the south seas to the eternal reproach of those who first brought it among them.' Like this infection, other diseases were later to follow and spread like fire throughout the islands and the islanders. But it was not only new diseases that Europeans brought, and to which the islanders were so susceptible. They also brought new tools, new animals, new ideas and a new morality. Girls found it hard to resist the strange nails offered to them by the sailors. Soon they demanded two, three or even four nails in exchange for their affection. Before the end of Cook's first visit on Tahiti, a sailor had been flogged for stealing large quantities of nails from the ship's storeroom.

Cook was to return three times. He was followed by the Spanish, the British Captain Bligh in the *Bounty*, British missionaries, American sealers and whalers, and then the French. All these visitors – or intrusions – were to contribute to the transformation of the Tahitians. Whether through disease, alien codes of laws and morals, firearms, alcohol or trinkets, their contribution had nothing to do with the slow, natural rhythm of life on Tahiti as it had been lived until then. In the words of Alan Moorehead, it was a fatal impact.

At first, neither Cook nor the islanders saw things in this light. Cook was acting under orders from the British Admiralty and he was most scrupulous in his behavior towards the islanders. His desire was to make friends with them, and interfere as little as possible with the life of the Tahitians. But the contact between the white sailors and the dark islanders was a sharp and irrevocable turn in the history of the Pacific.

Tahiti was only a small dot in a vast ocean, a tiny parcel of land which barely covered 400 square miles. The slopes of the mountains, so high and dramatic they could be seen from 60 miles away at sea, were covered with thick tropical forest and on the flat shores below the Tahitians moved among groves of coconut and breadfruit trees. There were no villages. The huts, open on all sides to the breeze, were scattered about under the deep shade of the plantations, each about fifty yards from its neighbor. Although it lay in the tropics of the central Pacific, its hot damp climate was not oppressive; there were almost constant trade winds. There was fresh water in abundance from the mountain torrents; flowers and fruit grew everywhere. To 18th century sailors it must have appeared very close to paradise.

In Cook's day the brown, handsome Tahitians probably numbered about 40,000. Banks and others aboard the *Endeavour* wrote of their dark liquid eyes and perfect teeth, of the sprays of jasmine and hibiscus in their long black hair, and of their smiling welcoming faces. The Tahitians wore bright toga-like robes which, in the evening, or in the presence of important people, they dropped to the waist, male and female alike. The islanders struck Cook and the sailors as very clean, for they bathed three times a day and removed the hair from beneath their arms and their faces. But there were, to the European taste, certain imperfections: the Tahitians' noses were a little too flat; they tended to grow fat with age, they tattooed their bodies with black designs and they covered themselves with coconut oil which after a time turned rancid.

The islanders did little work. But there was no real necessity for it. The food grew all around them. There were fish in the lagoons, breadfruit and coconuts in the branches above their heads. Bananas, sugar cane and yams grew wild and small pigs and fowls were roasted in earth ovens for their feasts. To call these people lazy was a European judgement, for in Tahiti a morning spent gathering fruit or fishing was enough to provide food for two or three days. Arts and crafts, which took up much of their time, were simple and they had all the materials at hand: bark from the trees was beaten into cloth and colored with natural dyes, palm leaves were woven into mats and roofs for their huts, coconut shells were their drinking cups, and their canoes, 60 or 70 feet long with sails and outriggers, were made out of local timber. There were no snakes or dangerous animals to threaten them; earthquakes and hurricanes rarely came their way; they were illiterate and did not care.

Cook, the explorer on a casual visit, saw this as an idyllic life. But on a closer view it did have its compli-

Living off tourists' tips
by fulfilling the brochures
clichés is a way to survive
— but may threaten
one's self-respect.

cations and drawbacks. Tahitian society was divided into tribal groups, each with a ruling family surrounded by an upper class. Below these were the general mass of islanders and the servants or serfs – a division, in fact, not unlike the class structure of 18th century Europe. In youth, at least, promiscuity was general. But no woman of the ruling or upper class would have thought of offering herself to an English sailor except in the most unusual circumstances. The bonds of marriage, when entered, were strict. And although young girls, from the age of ten or so, would readily make love without modesty, most of them came from the lower class. When a girl became pregnant, her marriage normally followed. Only if the father was an English sailor who would or could not marry the girl would the chain break down.

Nor did the apparent good nature and amiability of the Tahitians prevent them from engaging in tribal wars. Six months before Cook arrived there had been a devastating battle between Big Tahiti (the larger end of the island) and Little Tahiti. Battles were often preceded and followed by human sacrifices, a prisoner or a serf being used as the victim. The privileged priesthood, the *arioi*, were also some way from innocence. Except for the very highest among them, whose children were judged to come from the gods, they were childless – not because of celibacy, but because their children were strangled at birth.

Two years after leaving Tahiti on his first Pacific voyage, Cook and his companions returned to England with idyllic descriptions of the Tahitians. Europe in the 1770s seems to have been ripe for just such a notion of an earthly paradise. Only 20 years before, Rousseau had written his *Discours sur les arts et sciences* and since that time Europe's imagination had been intrigued by his veneration of simple and unsophisticated man living in Arcady. The discovery of Tahiti was the apparent reality of a preconceived idea. Cook brought back proof that such a place and such men as noble savages did exist. His impressions were yet untarnished and he spoke of a golden isle inhabited by happy, healthy, beautiful people whose every want was supplied by the tropical forest and who, best of all, knew nothing of the fanciful notions of civilization.

There was, however, a paradox. For the presumption of European superiority had already reared its head in the Pacific among the simple islanders. This was almost certainly the most significant contribution of European explorers – with the exception of Cook and a number of others – to the fatal impact of civilization upon Pacific islands. On his second visit among the Tahitians Cook was compelled to write 'we debauch their morals already prone to vice and we introduce among them wants and perhaps diseases which they never before knew and which serve only to disturb that happy tranquility they

Cook's crew wrote of the islanders' dark liquid eyes and glossy black hair; they still keep shining and clean, bathing several times a day.

and their forefathers had enjoyed. If anyone denies the truth of this assertion let him tell what natives of the whole extent of America have gained by the commerce they had had with Europeans.' Throughout Cook was to show respect and tolerance for the ways of the Tahitians; his manners were rarely shared by others.

Uncertainty about the long-term effects and desirability of European contact grew rapidly. It was reflected not only in Cook's journals but also in the reaction to the official accounts of voyages in the Pacific. Diderot spoke for a large section of European opinion when, in his *Supplément au voyage de Bougainville* (about the voyages of Cook's French contemporary), he inveighed against tampering with the natural simplicity of the Tahitians and prophesied with great accuracy the effects of Christianity, disease and extended contact with western seafarers upon the fragile innocence of the islanders.

But strength of feeling by *philosophes* and their followers was not enough to halt the momentum of European involvement. On his second voyage Cook called twice at Tahiti, in August 1773 and in April-May 1774, and at once noticed the bleaker aspects of island life. Since his previous visit two civil wars had been fought, political intrigue was rife, there was little in the way of surplus provisions to be obtained. Venereal disease had become common and an epidemic of gastric influenza had swept the island after a Spanish ship had called at Tahiti. On his third voyage Cook discovered that the Spaniards had returned and not only claimed the island, but had left a party of missionaries for ten months before returning to pick them up. They had built a house, furnished it in a spartan manner, attempted to convert the natives to Christianity and warned the Tahitians against dealings with the British.

Civil war had occurred in Cook's absence and was pending again. Prices had risen greatly and the nails and other trinkets of the first voyage could buy neither favors nor provisions. Cook also introduced the first horses ever seen in Tahiti, and they caused a huge sensation. In general terms his impression of Tahiti from the third voyage was that the age of innocence was over – that the missionaries' era was rapidly approaching and that the initial respect for the white sailors had given way to an attitude of self-interest. Already the traditional arts and crafts were vanishing; islanders no longer used to make stone tools – nor probably knew how – despite the fact that there was no guarantee that their European iron ones would be replaced. Yet Cook equally knew that it was too late to go back 'to the happy mediocrity in which they lived before we discovered them.' Already Tahiti had become drawn into the orbit of western civilization. Cook indeed believed that having been responsible for this, Europe had to keep it up. He wrote in his journal: 'It seems to me that it has become, in a manner, incumbent on the Europeans to visit them once

in three or four years in order to supply them with those conveniences which we have introduced among them and have given them a predilection for . . .'

In a sense Cook was right, but those who came with goods to succour the islander's needs, came also to exploit; they did not come to preserve the native culture. The Spanish missionaries of 1774 were indeed the vanguard of the later and much more concentrated effort of the London Missionary Society. It is easy, with hindsight, to criticize the missionaries for their narrow zeal and total disregard for the native institutions which were fundamental to the islanders' lives. Yet they are no more guilty than Cook himself. They came to save souls, but adopted a culturally ruinous policy to do so. The missionaries were by no means the only villains of the piece, although villains they were in the accounts of latter-day Diderots. These cynics saw the missionaries' aims and methods as utterly alien to the Tahitian way of life, as corrupters of the islanders' characters and imposers of guilt where none had hitherto existed. The second wave of European interlopers – crews of whaling ships (up to 150 ships a year) then traders, beachcombers, and finally planters – institutionalized the western presence in a way that the tiny number of missionaries with their chronic lack of supplies and trade goods could never do. To some extent indeed the missionaries and the mercantile interests were in conflict.

The dissolution of Tahitian society followed steadily. Diseases, including tuberculosis and smallpox, brought death; alcohol brought the destruction of many traditional customs and pastimes, adding to the complete demoralization of the native population. It was a situation which could not be cured by simply singing Christian hymns. By the end of the 18th century the population of Tahiti had declined from 40,000 to 16,000 and by the third decade of the 19th century, it had fallen to 9,000. When Melville portrayed Tahiti in his books *Typee* and *Omoo*, and when Gauguin arrived there to paint, Tahitian society had lost almost all its traditional culture. The society that remained was only the decadent dregs of a culture that Europe, at first unwittingly, but later with full intent, destroyed by demoralization and never by force or arms. The political annexation of Tahiti and most of the Pacific islands was only the logical conclusion of the tragic decline of Polynesia into a poor and later neglected client of Europe. For Melville and for Gauguin the root of the evil was the deadening touch, not of western civilization itself, but of its representatives; with the notable exception of Cook, they had debased native culture but had supplied no viable alternative. Tahiti's fall from grace had been because of the tantalizing fruit offered by Europeans. The fall had begun even on the days when the sails of Bourgainville's and Cook's ships appeared over the hitherto eternally empty horizon.

When Cook first arrived,
Tahiti's girls danced for the
love of dancing. Then they
wanted nails. Now they get
hard cash from the gawpers.

On the Marquesas Islands
where Gauguin died, a farmer's
only possessions are unloaded
— mass-made chattels
from a borrowed culture.

Samoans
Polynesia

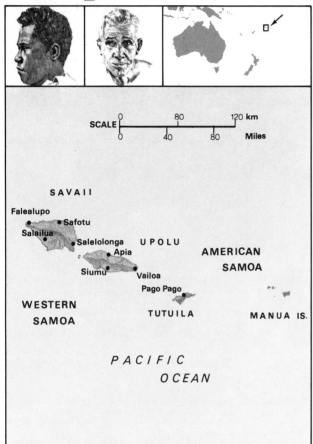

SCALE

SAVAII

Falealupo
Safotu
Salailua
Salelolonga
Apia
Siumu
Vailoa
UPOLU
AMERICAN SAMOA
Pago Pago
WESTERN SAMOA
TUTUILA
MANUA IS.

PACIFIC OCEAN

At dawn, the soft brown roofs of Samoan beehive houses and the slender tilting palm trees stand out against a colorless, gleaming sea. The life of the day begins at dawn, when the first shouts of young men may be heard from the hillside. Uneasy in the night that has been filled with the shadows of ghosts, the men shout lustily to one another as they hasten to their work. Lovers slip home from beneath palm trees or the darkness of beached canoes, that the light may find each sleeper in his appointed place. The cocks crow and shrill birds cry from the breadfruit trees. To the sounds of the waking village, the muted roar from the reef seems an undertone. Babies cry and restless little children roll out of their sheets to wander drowsily to the beach where they freshen their faces in the sea. Fires are lit here and there and the white smoke is hardly visible against the paleness of the dawn. The young men are called together by the sound of a rhythmic tattoo. Digging sticks in hand, they start inland for the cultivation plots of yams. Older men trudge off on lonely occupations. Women carry piles of washing to the spring, or set off inland to find weaving materials. Older girls go fishing off the reef while men in canoes slip out into the burning glare of the sun for the deep sea fish.

The village is awake. Women pause in their gossip to

45

After 100 years of colonial rule, Samoa remains essentially Samoan. The people prefer a simple life, *fa'a Samoa*, 'the ways of our fathers'.

Samoans Polynesia

In a Samoan village the
houses have no walls, only
blinds woven by girls. The
church, however, is a more
formal and modern building.

Once the years of caring for
her younger brothers and
sisters are over, a girl
thrusts away responsibility
with the words 'I am but young'

listen to the wail of a messenger who brings news of death in another village. Poor relatives whisper their heart's desire to richer relatives. Men make plans to set fish traps and questions are called out in their formal and respectful manner of speech: 'Is it bonito fishing your lordship is going?' (The language is a Samoan branch of Polynesian.) In the houses the pebbly floors are swept clean; old men sit apart from women nursing babies or great with child. Unceasingly the old men twist palm husk on their bare thighs and recount ancient tales in an undertone. Carpenters begin work on a new house while the owner bustles around to keep them happy; the carpenters are respected men. Taro, yams and bananas which have already been brought from the plantations are prepared for cooking on hot stones, for baking beneath a cover of banana leaves. A household cooks only once every two or three days and then the food is stored in baskets hung inside the house. As the sun rises higher in the sky, shadows deepen under the thatched roofs, the sand burns and flowers wilt; small children bid still smaller children to 'come out of the sun'. They bark instructions at their small charges; they are no more than six or seven years old and are not strong enough to lift

An adage on human dignity runs, if a tropic-bird loses its bright tail feathers, it loses its balance. West Samoan police take no chances.

the baby. Instead they carry their charge straddled on the hip. Mothers rarely exert themselves to discipline a young child if an older one can be made responsible.

The houses have no walls, only blinds woven by the girls from palm leaves. As the afternoon progresses and the sun slants, these blinds are let down and those remaining in the houses wrap their heads in sheets and go to sleep. A few adventurous children slip away for a swim in the shadow of a high rock. In the dazzling heat, the village falls silent until the sun begins to sink over the sea. Later, in the cool evenings, the sleeping are stirred for a second time that day. They may be roused by the cry of 'a boat, a boat!' as fishermen beach their canoes and spread the bright fish on the floors of their houses. Women pour water over them to free them of taboo, and regretfully the men turn out other species of fish that are taboo which must be presented to the village chief. Younger fishermen proudly pack small palm leaf baskets with fish for their sweethearts. Men in small groups begin to return from the plantations, carrying yams and calling as they come. Later they gather in the guest house for an evening of kava drinking; their softly clapping hands and the high pitched voice of the Talking Chief who serves the kava echoes through the village. Finally the sun sets in a deep glow and the last bathers come up from the beach and children straggle home. Lights shine out from the houses where everyone gathers for the evening meal. In front of a house at the end of the village a father cries out the birth of a son. Young men go off to give presents to their lovers. Honored guests are served first at the meal. In some houses a face is missing: a child has gone to the house of a relative, a girl has taken refuge with her uncle because her father was too strict.

After supper the old people and the little children are bundled off to bed. The night is the time for lighter things than councils of old men and the labors of babies. If the young people have guests, the front of the house is given over to them. If it is a moonlit night, then groups of two or three may wander through the village while gangs of children chase each other through the towering breadfruit trees or hunt for land crabs which scuttle in the pale darkness. Many from the village may take canoes out into the curving lagoon and fish by torchlight, sprinkling the water with wavering lights and shouts of triumph or disappointment. Often sleep and silence do not descend on the village until long past midnight. And even then the silence is incomplete. There is always the thunder from the reef to accompany the muted whispers of lovers.

There may be thirty or forty households in a Samoan village, each presided over by a *matai* or headman. In the village, the headmen hold either chiefly titles or the titles of Talking Chiefs who are official orators, the spokesmen and the ambassadors of chiefs. But in the household, whatever his title, the *matai* has complete authority over all who live for any length of time under his roof. A household may vary from only parents and children in 47

A West Samoan corporation has introduced Hereford cattle to the islands – but most West Samoans prefer taro and yams and other native foods.

(Bottom) In US Samoa, the village high chiefs preserve many of their traditional functions; the American colonial hand rests lightly.

After a long morning fishing and weaving the grown-ups sleep through afternoon heat. But the young slip out for a refreshing game in a waterfall.

one house, to fifteen or twenty people in two or three houses who are all related to the *matai* or his wife by blood, marriage or adoption. The adopted members are usually, but not necessarily, distant relatives.

All households are fluid and although the relationship between each member is demanding – for the youngest must always suffer the demands or criticisms of his or her elders – there are compensations. A child can wander safely and always be sure of finding food and drink, or a sheet to take a nap in. Any small children missing when night falls are sought at the houses of their kinsfolk. A baby whose mother has gone inland to the plantation may be passed from relative to relative the entire length of the village. And then there is also the freedom of each child or adolescent to move from the household of demanding parents to that of a less demanding relative. Few children live continuously in one house; they may move under the guise of visits with no suggestion of truancy. The possibility of a child's flight always tends to moderate the discipline or anger of parents. So cheerful is this system of refuge that an untitled man will defy his nobler relative who comes to demand a runaway child. With great politeness and endless apologies he will beg his noble chief to return to his noble home and remain there quietly until his noble anger is healed against his noble child.

Throughout the Samoan village, conventions and manners, respect for higher rank and for elders govern all relationships between the people. The visit of one Samoan to the house of another is not recognized until the correct speeches have been made. The visitor may, at first, be ignored by the household who continue with their chores until they are ready. Then one of them may spread a mat for the visitor; the guest arranges himself cross-legged on the mat, but sits in silence until his host has made a welcoming speech. If the guest is a white man, a *palangi*, he will thereafter be treated according to his appropriate Samoan rank. A common seaman, for example, would be treated as titleless. A professional man, an officer or official would be given a chiefly rank – especially if his own behavior is polite and dignified.

Similar conventions must be observed between relatives who visit each other's houses. If a man of low rank visits the house of a relative with higher rank, he is often suspected of seeking a favor or a gift; and although this is not frowned upon, for it is a man's right to make claims upon the property of his relative, a man is always reticent and delicate in his approaches; the object of his visit is only revealed after many hours. He may come to his relative's house early in the morning and enter quietly, then sit at the back in the place of least honor. His host may say to him 'So you have come, be welcome' and he will answer 'I have come indeed, saving your noble presence.' Then his host will continue 'Are you thirsty? Alas for your coming, there is little that is good within the house' and he will answer 'Let it rest, thank you, for

indeed I am not hungry, nor would I drink.' All day he will sit and make no mention of the purpose of his visit. He will brush ashes from the hearth, performing this menial task with great care. And he sits and studies his host's expression wondering if his request will be met favorably. He plays with the children but refuses the necklace of flowers they have woven for him and gives it instead to his host's daughter. Finally night comes and it is time to sleep, and he makes no move to go, nor to speak his mind. At last his host says with archaic formalism 'Lo, I would sleep. Would you sleep also, or will you be returning whence you have come?' Only then does he speak.

From a relative, a man may ask for food, clothing and shelter, or assistance in a feud. Refusal of any of these demands would brand the relative, whatever his status, as stingy and lacking in human kindness – the virtue most respected and sought after by all Samoans. Repayment of any favor or gift is not made at any particular time, no definite period is agreed except in the case of food distribution to all those who share in a family enterprise. Nevertheless, careful count is kept of these things in the Samoan mind; the value of any service or property given is demanded in return at the earliest opportunity. But the two acts, the one of initial 'begging' and the reciprocal act of asking for something in return, are quite separate. Each man, in turn, becomes a beggar. In the past the beggar sometimes wore a special girdle which hinted at the cause of his visit.

The *matai*, who is head of the household and to whom all requests are addressed, is exempt from the perform-ance of daily domestic tasks. However, except in the case of a high-ranking chief, the *matai* seldom takes advantage of this. Like all his junior relatives he works, taking the leading role in any agricultural or industrial pursuit. He dresses the pig for the feast. He cuts up the coconuts gathered by the boys and the women. The family cooking is shared between the women and the men, though in practice most falls upon the boys. Old men in the household spin the coconut fibers into braided cord which is used for fishing lines and nets and to sew parts of the canoes together; and with the old women who weave and make bark cloth for their clothes, they watch over the younger children who remain at home.

On the plantation, which lies inland from the village, much of the heavy work is done by the women. They weed and transplant, gather and carry home the food. They gather the paper mulberry wands from which bark is peeled for making bark cloth, tapa, and pandanus leaves which are used to weave their mats. Women and the older girls also do much of the reef fishing for octopus, sea eggs, jellyfish and crabs. Younger girls are given the task of carrying water up from the spring, and caring for the lamps which burn kerosene instead of the traditional candle-nut or coconut oils, and sweeping the pebble floors of the houses. All the tasks are ranked, and house-

hold members from the youngest to the oldest are allotted them according to their abilities. Often a task is rejected by a boy or a girl because a younger person has enough skill to perform it: it is not because any task is beneath a man's dignity.

The rank to which a child is born in a Samoan village will depend on the rank of his father, and throughout his life this will be of great importance. But to a child rankings are usually of less concern than the temper of an old woman or the demands of his mother. The village rank of the father barely affects the children except where he is a high chief or a high Talking Chief. In these households there is a greater emphasis on ceremony and more emphasis on hospitality. Later, as the child grows to an adolescent and then to a young man, rank not of birth but of title becomes more important. The status of a whole village depends on the rank of its chief, and similarly the prestige of a household depends on the title of its *matai*. Each title, whether chief or Talking Chief carries its own responsibilities and obligations apart from those owed to the household. The Samoans even have an elaborate courtesy language which must be spoken to people of rank. Among these people rank and prestige are a never-failing source of interest.

In the wider sphere of politics, where villages or islands

(Top) The capital of US Samoa, Pago Pago, has sophisticated television. Perhaps fortunately, electricity has not yet reached the bulk of the people.

There is an over-population problem in US Samoa: a shortage of land for farming has encouraged new fish canning industries.

Pago Pago, finest harbor in
the Pacific, grew up as a US
naval base. The Navy's
withdrawal after 1945 left
a big unemployment problem.

Samoans Polynesia

The meeting of chiefs in a
fale tele or ceremonial house
is called a *fono*: each chief
is given kava and a fixed
place according to his rank.

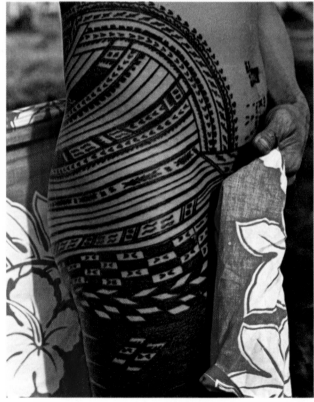

Once all young boys faced the
painful tattooing ceremony,
but today less than half
are tattooed and the ritual
has no connection with puberty.

(Top) A craftsman carves a long-legged kava ceremonial bowl. In this bowl, kava is passed round at all ceremonial meetings and visits.

Tapa, a bark cloth decorated with intricate designs, is made from the pounded and beaten bark of the paper mulberry tree.

come together in traditional alliances or confederations, the highest ranking chiefs gather in a *fono* or district council. The *fono* may be a meeting only of chiefs of a single village, or of a single island, and there have been frequent disputes between the major chiefs over the succession to the headship of Samoa. Although this is a position of great ceremonial and traditional power, it has little real political significance. Since Europeans asserted their authority on the islands of the Samoa group, there has been a decline in the effective power of chiefs. But ceremony and all its attendant activities is an undying element in Samoan village life. At the meetings of a *fono* or on the occasion of a *malanga* (a formal visit to another village), rules of precedence and the drinking of kava – or *ava* as the drink is known in Samoa – are part of elaborate rituals. During a *malanga*, fine mats woven from pandanus leaves by the women are exchanged. Gifts of food are made and the Talking Chiefs make speeches which are followed by a feast where the food is divided up according to the rank of each individual. Invariably a *malanga* is taken as an excuse to hold a *sivasiva*, a dance in which the young men and the young girls take over the ceremonial house while their elders, the married villagers and the chiefs, move to the back.

In many villages the center of all ceremonial functions is the *taupo*, a young girl, the daughter of a chief. At a *malanga* she dances for the visitors and is danced to by the young men. Mats are only exchanged in honor of her name or on the occasion of her marriage. And it is the *taupo* who is most important in the preparation of kava and its distribution. But women, though dominated by their chiefs, also have another institution to which they can attach themselves. This is the *aualuma* in which women whose husbands are dead, or who have no title (for a wife's rank depends upon that of her husband) or who are yet unmarried gather during ceremonies or act as hostesses during a *malanga*. Titled women, on the other hand, imitate their husbands and attend their own *fono* at which they drink kava and adopt the exact status of their husbands. Thus the chief's wife becomes the chief, the Talking Chief's wife, the speech-maker.

What is so remarkable about life in a Samoan village is that these things have not been rejected in favor of the technology and social practices of the European. The labors of missionaries have persuaded most of the Samoans to turn to Christianity. But side by side with this new religion, the less overt aspects of Samoan supernaturalism survive. The nights are still filled with *atua*, ghosts who have power over the living. And yet the new influences of the European have drawn the teeth of the old Samoan culture. Cannibalism, war, blood revenge, the life and death power of the *matai*, the enormous loss of life in making long voyages in small canoes, the discomforts of widespread disease – all these have vanished. And as yet their counterparts in producing misery have not yet appeared.

53

Tongans
Polynesia

In rank-conscious Tonga modes of speech vary according to the person addressed. At the top of society stand big King Tupou IV and his wife.

The Tongan archipelago, or the Friendly Islands as Captain Cook christened them, lie scattered over 20,000 square miles of the south Pacific Ocean a thousand miles north of New Zealand. Of the 150 islands less than 40 are inhabited. The total population is 90,000, some of whom, at the extremes of the archipelago, live as far as 200 miles from their nearest neighbors. They are an exceptionally handsome people, well built, proud of stature and bulk. Slim western women coming to the islands may receive from warmhearted Tongans openly expressed condolences for the misfortune of scragginess. Tongans are Polynesian, but have a distinctively Tongan 55

All members of the family
live under the same roof.
When father and mother go
out to work, grandmother
cares for the babies.

way of life. The islands are green and pleasant. The
Friendly Islands are a congenial habitat.

The history of the Tongans has not always been
characterized by a spirit of friendship. The Tongans have
a long, battle-scarred history of civil war and slavery.
According to Tongan traditions, the people came to their
islands from Samoa and the first chiefly dynasty was
founded about one thousand years ago. Recent research
has shown it is more likely that Tonga was inhabited long
before then. Tonga was probably the first of the present-
day Polynesian islands to be inhabited—some three
thousand years ago. Those early settlers brought with
them a culture that included decorated pottery which
persisted in Tonga for 1,500 years. There also survive
ancient pyramid-shaped tombs of kings, and burial
mounds, and midden dumps which tell what food the
pre-historic Tongans ate.

The Tongans were good navigators and well-practised
in the art of canoe building. They sailed widely throughout the archipelagos of central Polynesia and conquered
and controlled the peoples of many other islands. For
several hundred years they made slaves of the Samoans.
Then, in the 17th and 18th centuries, the voyages of
European explorers, including Tasman, brought Tongans
into contact with a new world. The visitors gained a
favorable impression of their hosts. They found them a
hospitable, orderly, peace-loving people, who respected
women and abhorred cannibalism. Captain Cook paid
three visits to Tonga in 1773, 1774 and 1777 and on his
last visit was so impressed by their welcome that he gave
them their name the Friendly Islands. Or so he thought.
He was not to discover until after this visit that, at what he
had taken to be yet another lavish celebration in his
honor, he had in fact narrowly escaped an abortive
assassination plot. The Tongans did not even pretend to
welcome the Christian evangelists when they arrived to
convert them. Christianity was regarded with a cold eye
by Tongan chiefs and priests.

Today the Tongans are as devoted in their adherence,
as they were once in their opposition, to Christianity.

They are dedicated, churchgoing, Sabbatarian Christians. The majority are Wesleyan Methodist; the rest are Roman Catholic, Anglican, Seventh Day Adventist and Mormon.

Throughout their history the Tongans have had continuous contact with the Fijians. They intermarried with them and continue to do so today. From the fierce and warlike Fijians they got their large canoes, and their taste for fighting. Civil war broke out between the three branches of the royal family early in the 19th century and the community was torn apart with prolonged and heavy fighting. It was a protracted struggle that turned the Tongans' society from scattered settlements into village groups offering refuge and security. By the 19th century, when the missionaries came, villages were common and Tongan communities were potentially easy to group around a church. The Tongan initial resistance to conversion found new outlets in fierce competition between the villages as to whose village church was the biggest and most splendid.

But it was Taufa'ahau, also known as King George Tupou I (after King George III of England) who finally unified Tonga under his rule in 1845. He and his wife Salote (the Polynesian version of Charlotte – after Queen Charlotte) had been baptised in 1831. He laid sound

Landing is always hazardous on volcanic Niuafo'ou – or Tin Can Island, so called after its method of postal delivery and collection.

(Top) On Niuafo ou Tongans carry copra to the beach from their old-fashioned houses made of the bark and leaf of coconut palms.

Tongans Polynesia

A dead woman lies in state
in her home. Before burial
she will be wrapped in tapa
cloth and mummified. After
lamentation comes feasting.

foundations for the future of Tonga. He preserved the Tongan monarchy, but gradually shifted much of its power to a form of constitutional government. He abolished serfdom and instituted a system whereby every Tongan was guaranteed a plot of land of about eight acres called an *api*, and also a site for his house in a village.

Almost every Tongan today has a house and land of his own. Tongan houses are built in a cluster. They have thatched roofs, reed walls and earthen floors. Beyond lie the fields, cut out of the forest, where the peasant farmers cultivate yams, sweet potatoes, maize, taro (a root crop), sugar cane and pandanus; they also grow fruits like mangoes, pineapples and papaya, breadfruit, bananas and coconuts. Like most other Pacific islanders, the Tongans also cultivate the kava plant from which they make a mildly narcotic drink; they raise chickens and pigs, and fish from the sea that is all around them. The Tongans are self-sufficient. Wells have now been dug and pipes laid which avert the threat of drought during the dry season and its irregular rains.

The Tongans' most feared enemy is the hurricane. A hurricane will destroy any coconut palm or banana plant in its path – and on these two crops, bananas and copra, Tonga's cash economy is based. The integrity of the Tongans as a people is reinforced by their monarchy's pledge never to sell a square foot of Tongan soil to outsiders – a pledge respected by Britain in her colonial role. Foreigners may only lease land from the government, and only with government approval. There is every likelihood that on Tonga, unlike a number of other island groups in the Pacific, the social life of the islands will flourish without major changes in the social structure for generations to come. Even the beating of tapa (bark cloth) into huge decorated sheets shows no sign of vanishing from Tonga.

Tongan society is dominated by a highly developed consciousness of rank. More than in any other Pacific community the importance of rank and a man's inherited position affects every aspect of Tongan life. Tonga is the smallest kingdom on earth. It is also the last surviving south sea monarchy and its monarch is a direct descendant of the world's oldest reigning dynasty. The Tongan sense of rank is expressed every time a Tongan opens his mouth. If, for example, he uses the word 'go' in conversation with a king, he will say *há'ele*; if he is talking to a chief he will say *me'a*, and to a common man he will say *'alu*. The ceremonial attendants of the king are accordingly the traditional speech-makers and they are especially well-versed in the language of respect.

Whenever two Tongans come together they are careful to establish their respective rank, of which there are two distinct varieties.

One kind of social rank distinguishes chiefs and commoners. Within this structure are various refinements, for example, the *matapule* (half-way chiefs or ceremonial attendants). Then there are distinctions between legal chiefs and traditional chiefs – a complication arising from the second variety of social rank based on descent from the very first king of the present dynasty, Tui Tonga. Tui Tonga's father, Ahoeitu, was born in extraordinary circumstances. He was the offspring of the god Tangaloa Eitumatupua, who climbed down from the sky on a great casuarina tree, with a woman from an earlier Tongan population descended from a worm. When Ahoeitu, who was half-man and half-god, was old enough he went up into the sky to visit his celestial father, and brought back with him to earth several celestial people who became his *matapule*. Ahoeitu, according to legend, lived more than one thousand years. The succeeding Tui Tonga were all descended from him.

In the 15th century the 24th Tui Tonga appointed his younger brother as subsidiary ruler. They ruled alongside each other, the elder, the Tui Tonga, reserving the spiritual authority of the representative of the gods while

On Niuatoputapu and on most Tongan islands, horse-drawn carts outnumber trucks and cars.

(Top) Five Wesleyan priests conduct a burial service, while Tongan mourners, each with black tapa mats round the waist, solemnly assist.

59

To express respect for grand visitors, Tongans cover the road with tapa mats. Here Tongatapu islanders await British royalty.

(Bottom) Tongan children enjoy Sunday church. A priest looks on as children enact scenes from the Bible.

the younger brother ruled the people. And thus a second chiefly line, the Tui Ha'atakalaua, was created. It became a custom for the Tui Tonga to take as his principal wife the eldest daughter of the Tui Ha'atakalaua. The rank of the eldest daughter of this marriage was higher than that of her father or brother, the succeeding Tui Tonga, and indeed was so high that men of only two great chiefly families were worthy of marrying her. The rank of her daughter would in turn be so high, that not even her own mother was sufficiently exalted to eat in her presence.

In the 16th century the Tui Ha'atakalaua, the temporal ruler, whether through a feeling of superiority or of laziness, delegated the actual work of government to a younger son, thereby creating a third chiefly line, the Tui Kanokupolu. Now there were three chiefs, all descended from Ahoeitu and all related by marriage. Eventually the second line lost its status while the third line grew more powerful. It was rivalries between these chiefs which caused the 19th century civil wars – in one of which the last reigning Tui Ha'atakalaua was killed. The chief of the third line, King George Tupou I, won.

Although his supremacy was assured when the last Tui Tonga died in 1865 the rank inherent in the other two chiefly dynasties did not die. And it is this which makes the seemingly simple Tongan social distinction between chiefs and commoners so complicated. The rank of the living descendants of the other two chiefly dynasties was, according to tradition, still higher than that of the king and his descendants. This dilemma was resolved by appointing men and women of these two other chiefly lines to new ranks, with new titles. Frequent inter-marriage has today made the three lines almost equal. It is a complexity which touches the life of every Tongan. A major preoccupation is the working out of one's descent and of one's relationship with any of the three chiefly lines which lead ultimately to descent from the half-god Ahoeitu himself.

The matter is further complicated for Tongans by ranking within the family itself. Within any Tongan family – for which there is no word except *káinga*, which means kinsmen – all relations are called *káinga* and treated according to their rank in the group. Sex is more important than age and sisters have a higher rank than their brothers. This can have, to western eyes, bizarre results: brothers, for example, often avoid their sisters; and a girl of twelve may be senior to her 25 year old brother.

Another principle, and another social complication, of *káinga* rank gives precedence to kinsmen related through the father. Taking all these principles together, the Tongan's highest kin is thus his father's eldest sister. After her come his father's other sisters, and then the father's brothers according to their age. The lowest rank of all is the lot of the mother's brothers. His sisters' children have a higher status than he has, while his own children – whether boys or girls – and those of his

The explorer Cook called
Tonga the Friendly Isles.
Friends here share a
fine meal of sucking
pig roasted over a spit.

brothers, are lower down the scale.

Occasionally someone may rank higher than another person on the basis of descent from Ahoeitu and relationship to the three chiefly lines, but lower on the basis of kinship. Sometimes two people may be related in two different ways, and they may alternately outrank each other. Tongans avoid embarrassment in these situations by taking seniority in turns.

By whatever system of rank, so high-faluting do some people in Tonga became that they outrank all others and can find no fellow Tongans worthy of marrying them. For such people there is nothing but to make a Fijian match. The late Queen Salote's father, King Tupou II, had just this problem and resolved it by taking a Fijian wife. Marriages between Tongans and Fijians have created a new social group, the *Fale-Fisi*.

The rules which govern inheritance in a Tongan *káinga* are not those which govern status. Women may socially have higher status, but they inherit nothing from their fathers. Land, which is wealth in this nation of peasant proprietors, passes from father to son – although there is a modern tendency for a man's widow also to inherit land. The eldest son, the inheritor, becomes the head of the family, expected to look after his brothers until they can obtain their own land, and care for his sisters until they are married.

The most important events for Tongan people and their *káingas* are weddings and funerals. It is on these occasions, and on days of national importance, that titles are conferred and high-ranking men change their status. All a man's relatives gather for his funeral. The relatives with a higher status, who are related through his father, remain near the corpse. Here they wail, accept gifts from other relatives and drink kava. Women prepare tea and bread and everyone eats it there and then. Later food which has been cooked in the earth ovens is distributed, wrapped in coconut leaf baskets. Cooking and serving food is thought a menial task in Tonga, but at the funeral of his father's sister, even the highest chief must prepare an earth oven. The mourning may go on for months.

Official mourning lasted six months after the funeral in 1965 of the late Queen Salote, an affair which concerned the whole of Tonga, every chief and every *káinga*. Not only did every Tongan wear black, but there were no parties, no dancing or singing, no beating of tapa into vast decorated sheets, no films and little noise until a huge kava ceremony ended the period of mourning. Two years later, Tongans gathered together again for another event which absorbed all Tongans, from even the furthest flung islands of the archipelago. This time it was a happy occasion – the installation of King Tupou IV.

61

Hawaiians
Polynesia

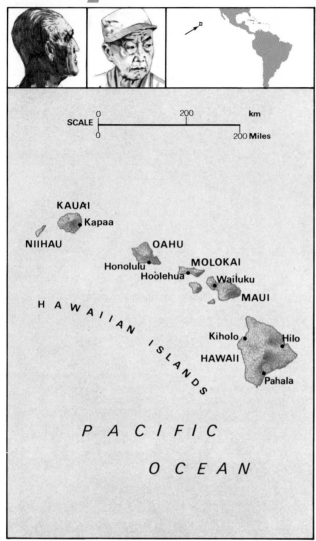

One day the demi-god Maui went out fishing and caught his nets on the ocean floor. He gave what must have been a mighty pull, for up came not fish but eight islands: Niihau, Kauai, Oahu, Molokai, Lanai, Maui, Kahoolawe, and Hawaii. His remarkable haul in fact comprised the main Hawaiian group of islands. This was the Polynesian legend. Today schoolchildren in Hawaii are taught that their islands are volcanic in origin, and that the land on which they live is in fact the tops of an under-sea mountain range which extends almost 2,000 miles from north to south. However they came to be there, these islands at the northern tip of the Polynesian triangle are often called the 'Paradise of the Pacific' for their beauty, for their climate, and for the warmth of their people. The Hawaiians themselves are aware of their good fortune. 'Hawaii no ka oi' – 'Hawaii is the best' – has long been a commonplace saying

62

The new world mesmerized by the old: US tourists are entranced by the lithe and provocative grace of hula dancers in grass skirts.

Honolulu's Waikiki Beach, the
most crowded in the world,
was once a sleepy bungalow
town between great green
mountains and limpid sea.

among Hawaiians.

Visitors seem to agree. More than a million people
visit Hawaii each year, and tourism – the entertainment,
hotel, souvenir, and travel industries – provides a massive
annual revenue. Up to the 1930s most visitors to the
islands arrived by ship. Coming into Honolulu Harbor,
they were greeted by one of the loveliest sights on earth:
the great green mountains that drape the center of Oahu
like a curtain, majestic Diamond Head, and the white
surf breaking on the beach of a sleepy bungalow town
called Waikiki. This famous beach is now lined with
hotels, and during the peak holiday season Waikiki has
a population density of 74,814 people per square mile,
which is higher than that of New York's Manhattan.
Many visitors have been so taken with the island that
they have returned to settle there. The population of
Honolulu, the capital, has doubled since World War II.
The original population has long been swamped in
members and culture and Oahu's urban growth problems are often cited as an object lesson for those Pacific
islands where commercial development is still embryonic.
Today, Hawaii is an American place, with an original
Hawaiian garnishing. The majority of the people are
Japanese or white Americans.

The outer islands have fortunately been less affected
by the problems of overdevelopment. Life out here
moves at a slower pace. There are few hotels and instead
of freeways, more intimate roads wind among the hills,
the sub-tropical runs wild, and the long views are un-
marred by concrete towers. The towns are small, and
the houses of a kind that has almost disappeared from
Honolulu – rambling wooden bungalows with large
verandas, set in gardens of brilliant *ti* plants and hibiscus
bushes. Barefoot children run all over the place. It is
unlikely that these islands will ever be developed as
Oahu has been, but the past two hundred years have seen
so many changes in the group as a whole that many have
wondered if the 'Old Hawaii' is still there.

To white residents 'Old Hawaii' means the days of a
generation and more before the hotels, before the apart-
ment buildings, and before the Japanese attack on Pearl
Harbor in December 1941 brought the US into World
War II. These were the days when everyone would go
down to greet the cruise liners whether they knew anyone
aboard or not, and few doors were ever locked. To the
visitor 'Old Hawaii' means grass skirts and grass houses –
the stuff of today's touristic clichés.

First Hawaiians arrived in great sea-going canoes
which they paddled, navigating by the stars from
'Havaiki', the Polynesian homeland in the south – pro-

Hibiscus and *ti* blossoms
make garlands for Lei Day on
May 1st: a flower worn behind
the right ear means that
the wearer wants a lover.

(Bottom) Hawaii is a racial
melting pot: 28% are white
American, 30% Japanese; the
rest are Chinese or 'mixed'
— only a fraction true Hawaiian.

bably Tahiti – a distance of 3,000 miles. Over the next
two hundred years more canoes made the voyage, bringing not only settlers but also the plants and domesticated
animals of the south Pacific: taro, sweet potato, breadfruit, yams, bananas, coconuts, sugar cane, pigs, chickens,
and dogs. By 1300 AD the voyages had stopped. For
some five hundred years Hawaii was entirely free of
foreign influence or domination.

Society was relatively uncomplicated. The climate and
the abundance from the sea made possible a leisurely
way of life where work could often be put aside for play.
'Uku pau' the Hawaiians would say – 'we have worked,
now we will do something else.' Life was lived out of
doors – the grass houses were mainly for sleeping – and
most of the villages were on or near the beaches where the
canoes could be drawn up on the sand and the great nets
were spread to dry. The men tended the taro patches,
cleared the sweet potato and yam fields, and fished the
reefs and bays with nets, lines and lures. The women
gathered seaweed and shellfish from the rocks, tended
the animals, and collected tart berries like the *ohelo* for
relishes. Their dishes and cooking methods survive today.
They ate some seafood raw, but most foods were cooked
in the rock-lined pits in the ground called *imus*. A large
pig might take an entire night to cook, but the slow process always produced succulent food with a tantalizing
smoky taste. All meals included a large quantity of *poi*,
a thin paste prepared by pounding baked taro roots
mixed with water. Everything was eaten with the fingers
including the *poi*. The consistency of a batch of *poi* was
described by the number of fingers required to convey a
portion to the mouth, so that you could have one-finger
poi, two-finger *poi*, and so on.

The women made tapa cloth for skirts and loincloths
from the inner bark of the paper mulberry, which they
beat into thin sheets and decorated with geometrical
designs in bright natural dyes. No-one wore shoes except
on journeys over rocky terrain, when they wore sandals
of plaited *ti* leaf or *lauhala* (pandanus), which the women
also plaited into mats and baskets. Both men and women
wear *lois* (garlands) of shells, nuts, dogs' teeth, flowers
or *maile* vines in their hair and around their necks,
wrists, and ankles.

There were many temptations to say *'Uku pau'* – foot
races, boxing, a form of bowls and darts and *kilu*, a
game for two in which the forfeit was a kiss. There were
diving contests, swimming and canoe races, and surfing,
'the sport of kings' – so called because only the chiefs
and chieftainesses were allowed to use the large surf-
boards which could carry their standing riders half a
mile on the crest of a wave. The commoners used short
body-boards, or body-surfed the inshore waves like
otters. It was the Hawaiians who developed the *hula*
dance.

There were several hundred named spirits, and many
of the chiefs also had special family guardian deities

65

Lei flowers commemorate the
tragedy of Pearl Harbor,
which marked the passing of
'Old Hawaii': traditions are
only intact on outer islands.

(*akua*) who watched over members of the family and
protected them in times of danger. The *akua* were particularly held in awe, and their existence was often kept
secret. It was considered dangerous to profane their
names by uttering them outside the family. One such
was Io or Iolani, the hawk-god of the ruling Kamehameha
family. The hierarchy of deities includes gods of war,
light, harvest and volcanoes. The pig possessed an
element of sanctity, and was the chosen form of one of
the more influential spirits. There was a strong belief in
a tribe of elves who allegedly lived in the mountains and
were said to perform amazing and miraculous feats
by night.

If life was easy in some ways, it was hard in others, for
traditional Hawaiian society was a rigid hierarchy of
three castes: the nobility *(ali'i)*, the priests *(kahuanas)*,
and the commoners. The *ali'i*, the chiefs, claimed descent
from the gods. Women could be chiefs in their own right.
Relations between *ali'i* and commoners were proscribed
by the elaborate series of religious taboos called the *kapu*
system: a commoner who inadvertently remained standing in the presence of a chief, touched him or his clothing,
or approached him from behind, would instantly be put
to death.

The *kahunas* were often members of the nobility whose
sacred occupation enabled them to exercise power over

Missionaries tried to put
stiff Mother Hubbard dresses
on beautiful Hawaiian girls,
but they soon adapted them to
more seductive shapes.

Fish and piglet, smoky from cooking in the ground, fresh pineapple and coconut with *poi* paste, and Polynesian hospitality make up a feast.

the *ali'i* and commoners. Rulers were advised by *kahuana nuis* (chief priests), and the favors of the gods could be withdrawn if the desires of their priests were not satisfied. The *kahunas* could demand special levies of food or goods for religious festivals; they collected the human sacrifices which certain of the gods required, and they were responsible for ensuring that people who violated the *kapus* received their punishment. One *kapu* that must often have been violated was the one which governed eating: men and women were not allowed to eat together, and women were forbidden to eat pork, bananas, coconuts, and some kinds of seafood. The privileged classes existed at the expense of the commoners who were not allowed to own land, were obliged to work the land of their chiefs and supply the *ali'i* and *kahuanas* with food, fish, clothing, and military service, and might at any time be seized for sacrifice at one of the temples or simply killed for no reason other than the whim of a capricious chief.

The islands contained several chiefdoms, each ruled by a supreme chief called the *ali'i aimoku*. The *ali'i aimoku* might also be the *ali'i kapu* (chief of highest rank), but more often he had won his position through personal merit and ability against less able *ali'i* of higher rank. The *ali'i aimoku* owned all the land in his chiefdom, and divided it between his subordinate chiefs on the understanding that he might take it back at any time. Because there was no strict rule of succession, and because subordinate chiefs were always anxious to better their positions, there were frequent wars both within and between chiefdoms.

Four large chiefdoms had emerged from these wars by 1778, when Captain Cook discovered the group and renamed it the 'Sandwich Islands' in honor of the Earl of Sandwich. For ten years no ships visited the islands, wars were fought almost incessantly, and Kamehameha, an *ali'i* from Hawaii, began to emerge as the most powerful chief in the group. By 1810 Kamehameha had subdued all opposition, and the islands were for the first time united under a single ruler.

Under Kamehameha the *ali'i* and *kahunas* were deprived of many of their former powers. The lot of the commoners was improved by the *mamalahoe kanawai* (law of the splintered paddle), which bestowed on them a certainty of life they had not previously enjoyed: 'Let the aged, men and women, and little children lie down in safety in the road.' Kamehameha set an example for the *ali'i* by working the land with his own hands, and in the course of his lifetime transformed the islands into the kingdom of Hawaii. The Kamehameha dynasty gave Hawaii eight kings and two queens, and few ruling houses have been as dedicated as the Kamehamehas to improving the lot of their subjects. The first Kamehameha remained faithful to the old gods, but after his death in 1819 his successor abolished the *kapu* system and broke the power of the *kahunas* by forbidding the worship of the ancient gods. The people of Hawaii had a Constitution by 1840, and by 1848 the right to own land was no longer a monopoly of the aristocracy.

The Kamehameha dynasty ruled Hawaii until 1893. In these years large land holdings were acquired by foreign settlers who established sugar and pineapple plantations and imported contract laborers from Portugal, China, Korea and Japan. When Queen Liliuokalani came to the throne in 1891 there were many who felt that the land controlled by foreigners should be returned to the Hawaiian people. Concerned to protect their interests, the settlers overthrew the monarchy and established the Republic of Hawaii, which was annexed as a territory of the United States in 1898, and granted full statehood on 21 August 1959.

The collapse of the Kamehameha dynasty and the Kingdom of Hawaii surprised few. Hawaii's strategic location and the potential importance of the complex of deep sea lochs that became known as Pearl Harbor made it almost inevitable that Hawaii should be secured by one of the larger powers. Colonization was a fact of 19th century life. Some of the old Hawaiians said knowingly that it had come about through the hubris of the Kamehamehas who had taken the name of their god lightly and called their jewel-like royal palace 'Iolani'.

On the surface, there is much of the old Hawaii in the new. The old gods linger on as superstitions even among the newcomers. The goddess Pele is still thought to appear near the volcanoes on Hawaii when an eruption is at hand, and all *kamaainas* (long-time residents) know better than to carry pork on the road over Nuuanu Pali lest the god Kama-pua'a take offense. The recently imported American residents have adopted a smattering of Polynesian terms. Signs on private property say *'kapu'* instead of 'No Trespassing', and people give directions in Hawaiian: *'mauka'* (toward the mountain) or *'makai'* (toward the sea) instead of north or south. Troupes of dancing girls wear grass skirts for the sole benefit of the tourists, but the people of Hawaii long ago developed their own *mu'umu'u, holoku,* and *aloha* skirt from the first drab garments furnished by the missionaries. The *mu'umu'u* is a loose-fitting dress which is often short, and short-sleeved. The *holoku* was the favorite garment of the Hawaiian court of Edwardian times, and these elegant long dresses with trains are still worn to balls and formal occasions. The loose shirt with flowered patterns – now produced by more than eighty manufacturers – is a characteristic form of dress for the men. Such shirts are sold in great quantities to the tourists. Many reproduce, with variations, traditional patterns. There is a sizeable industry in souvenirs – imitations of ancient Hawaiian jewellery and the like. Tourists are taught the Polynesian code by which a flower worn behind the right ear means that you are looking, a flower behind the left that you are taken.

Many of the big hotels hold *luaus* (feasts) for the

Honolulu on Oahu Island by night — the Miami of the Pacific islands. Oahu's dramatic beauty has attracted too many people.

Buddhists light floating candles to guide spirits at the O'Bon Festival at Haleiwa and kimonoed Japanese girls dance in their honor.

Who's for hula? Visitors to Hawaii try to imitate this celebration of nature and sex whose sensuality so shocked 19th century visitors.

Guests relax at the Hilton hotel: tourism is a major industry and has replaced the spirit of *aloha* with the bell-hop mentality.

visitors, complete with *imu*-roasted pig – Churches hold *luaus* instead of fetes, and *kamaainas* give *luaus* to celebrate birthdays and weddings. All the foods of old Hawaii are available in the markets, and although *poi* is no longer pounded by hand it is still 'one-finger', or 'two-finger'. Many floors are covered with plaited *lauhala* mats, more suited to the climate and to bare feet than carpets. Children are sent to *hula* classes as children elsewhere go to ballet lessons, and there are canoe-racing associations instead of pony clubs. On '*Lei* Day' – 1 May – everyone wears at least one *lei* garland, and there are flowers everywhere. The *paniolos* (cowboys) on the great cattle ranches of Hawaii island wear feathers or flower *leis* on their stetson hats, and people still say '*Uku pau.*' The concern of the Kamehamehas for the welfare of the Hawaiian people is continued in the proud traditions of the Kamehameha Schools, founded in the 19th century by Princess Bernice Pauahi. Her will left her estates – almost 10 per cent of all the land in Hawaii – to provide an income for a school especially for children of Hawaiian ancestry.

It is, inevitably, a mongrelized culture, sustained by the constant flow of tourists, most of them from the US. Only the Polynesian heritage gives Hawaii any recognizable unity, and this is – again inevitably – so self-conscious and commercialized as to have been reduced to an elaborate gimmick. The only island of the group where anything more than a semblance of the traditional life is lived in Niihau, a 73-square-mile rock owned by a single family named Robinson. Here live some two hundred pure-blooded Hawaiians. However, this island is closed to all visitors except those personally invited by the Robinsons.

The original Hawaiian population was greatly reduced by epidemics in the early years of the last century. Leprosy took its toll: lepers were exiled to the island of Holokai; and it was then that Father Damica, the Belgian priest tending the lepers, finally himself succumbed to the disease. In the later part of the century, the population of the islands was swelling with the contract laborers from China, and Korea; the beginning of the great flood of Japanese was in 1868. When the contracts expired many laborers stayed to make their homes in Hawaii. They were replaced on the plantations by laborers from the Philippines, and moved into the towns where they built closely-packed little neighborhoods reminiscent of their original homes in Asia.

Honolulu's Chinatown was built during this period. Much of Chinatown has been demolished for urban renewal. Characteristically, an elegant cinema built to look like a Japanese castle looks across the banks of Nuuanu Stream towards a building whose tiled roof and

Bystanders in the brilliant
sunshine at Kapioli Park,
Waikiki, admire the skill
of local players of softball
which is very popular.

red columns entwined with dragons suggests vanished palaces of Peking. The first generation tried to maintain the traditional practices of the orient, but the system of arranged ethnocentric marriages was soon abandoned. Today over 40 per cent of the marriages performed in Honolulu, and 48 per cent of all babies born in Hawaii, are 'inter-racial'. A breakdown of the population by race shows that 28 per cent are Caucasian, 30 per cent Japanese, and 42 per cent Hawaiian, Chinese, Filipino, Korean, 'cosmopolitan' or 'inter-racial'. Today only one in six of the population claims to be wholly or predominantly Hawaiian.

Hawaii is called the melting pot not only because of the actual racial mixture, but also because of the mingling of cultures. The Hawaiians intermarried with the first foreigners. The last heir to the Hawaiian throne was half Scots. Of Honolulu's six daily newspapers, two are in English, two in Japanese and English, and two in Chinese. The language of the original inhabitants is current. The grandparents of the pretty girls who dance the *hula* for visitors might have come from Tokyo, Peking, Boston, or Luzon, and the girls might be named Kalani, Louise, Jade, or Tomiko. The traditional greeting on 25 December is *Mele Kalikimaka* (Merry Christmas), and on New Year's Eve the people turn out to see the Chinese dragons dance through the streets to the sound

of drums and firecrackers. During the *O-bon* Festival in August there are always crowds at the temples watching the Japanese dance in kimonos to honor the dead. Honolulu businessmen often wear elegant embroidered Filipino shirts with their dinner jackets, and on 5 March (Japanese Boy's Day) many non-Japanese households fly the paper carp that signify the number of sons in the family. Students at the Kamehameha Schools might be half Chinese or Filipino, many school-children go to classes after school to learn Chinese or Japanese calligraphy, and English – the *lingua franca* of Hawaii – is spoken with a lilting Hawaiian accent.

The hospitality for which Hawaii is famous is good for tourism. Yet its roots are in the character of the original inhabitants. The meaning of *aloha* embraces a philosophy of goodwill toward all men, of the importance of comradeship. It may be said on greeting, parting or as an expression of love. This warmth inherent in the original Polynesian character has affected the entire development of the mixed community that has supervened. Distant relationships are readily acknowledged. In the 19th century settlers were already tending to keep open house for visitors. While far from being incapable of feuding, Hawaiians have traditionally stressed the unity of their relatively small community – once two or three hundred thousand, and still under a million. The 71

The outrigger canoe links Hawaiians to their history and the first migrations of their people through Micronesia and the Society Islands to Hawaii.

Hawaiian adage runs: 'We are one family. We live together, work together, eat from the same calabash together – we are calabash cousins.'

Differences of race, class and income inescapably exist in today's community. Yet the spirit of Hawaiian unity is none the less a genuine one. The Japanese of the Hawaiian islands fought gallantly with the American army during World War II. On the return home to Hawaii, their vigorous confidence affronted many of the American settlers, who before the war had tended to regard the 'AJA' (Americans of Japanese ancestry) as second class citizens. The units in which they served – the 442nd Regimental Combat Team and the 100th Infantry Battalion – won an outstanding proportion of decorations; and of Hawaii's war dead, 80 per cent were of Japanese ancestry. It was President Harry Truman who first reacted to Hawaii's request for statehood, as the US's 50th state – a proposal which the AJA's war service did much to commend to the ordinary American voter. By the time that statehood was advanced in March 1959, the postwar resentment between the communities had largely disappeared. The preamble to the Hawaiian Constitution of 1840 begins with these words: 'God hath made of one blood all nations of men, to dwell on the face of the earth in unity and blessedness . . .' Though one of the world's most improbable multi-racial communities, it is indeed one of the most successful.

Surfing was once called the sport of kings because only chiefs and their wives were allowed the boards which bore them astride the massive waves.

Snow on towering Mauna Kea
on mainland Hawaii, where
islanders can both toboggan
and ski; some of the volcanic
peaks still erupt dramatically.

Tahitians
Polynesia

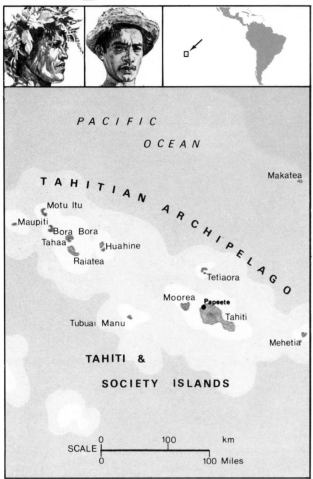

PACIFIC
OCEAN

Makatea

T A H I T I A N   A R C H I P E L A G O

Motu Itu
Maupiti
Bora Bora
Tahaa
Huahine
Raiatea

Tetiaora

Moorea
Papeete
Tahiti

Tubuai Manu

Mehetia

TAHITI &
SOCIETY ISLANDS

SCALE
0 ___ 100 ___ km
0 ___ 100 Miles

More than 12,000 books and articles have been written about Tahiti during the two hundred years that have elapsed since the discovery of this tropical island right in the middle of the Pacific Ocean. This is an astonishing number of publications for a small island, barely twice the size of the Isle of Man. The key word in most of the titles is paradise, and the authors vie with each other in praising the beautiful scenery, the mild climate and above all the wonderful hospitality and the easy, free life of the islanders, particularly the women. The pictures illustrating the text as a rule show a great number of invitingly smiling hula girls with bare bosoms, unavoidably creating the impression that the island is an earthly paradise, indeed an island inhabited by unabashed Eves, eagerly expecting to be tempted.

Dozens of prospective settlers, most of whom are men, write to me every month from Europe and America. Their purpose is not to enquire whether this frantically publicized image of Tahiti is true – because they are all equally convinced that it is – but simply to ask for the right addresses or for help with some practical details.

It is therefore of more than a purely theoretical interest

Materials for food, shelter
and clothing grow naturally
in Tahiti's tropical climate,
leaving the islanders with
time for the good things in life.

Many Tahitians, like this fisherman entering Cook's Bay, off Moorea, make their living catching tuna, bonito and swordfish.

left us excellent descriptions of the life and customs of the Pacific islanders.

These early navigators were all overwhelmingly impressed by the simplicity with which the Tahitians could satisfy the three universal human needs: for food, clothes and shelter. Thanks to the warm climate – the temperature stays perpetually in the vicinity of 85 degrees – and the abundant rains, particularly between October and March, the Tahitians can plant and harvest at almost any time of the year. Even more remarkable from the European point of view is that their crops hardly require any care at all. The most famous example is the breadfruit tree which can stand as a symbol of the type of simple subsistence economy that prevails in Tahiti. Six years after a sprout has been planted the tree begins to bear big, round fruits and continues to do so for the next fifty years. Each fruit, baked or roasted, provides food for one day for one person. Or let us take the equally famous coconut tree that in the same spontaneous manner produces nuts all the year round. Incidentally, contrary to a popular belief, it is not milk that you can drink straight from the nuts. The green drinking nuts contain only a clear liquid that must be called coconut water. Coconut milk is made by grating the kernel of a ripe nut and then squeezing out the white juice.

Only slightly greater efforts are needed to grow the remaining traditional vegetable foods: bananas, yams, taro roots and sweet potatoes. The attitude of the Tahitians toward the few domesticated animals they possessed at the time of the discovery – pigs, dogs and hens – was equally nonchalant. They let them run loose and fend for themselves. They ate the meat of all these three animals, but as they were scarce, only during important feasts. Fortunately they had another, richer and more easily available source of protein in the surrounding lagoon and ocean. Then as now the waters were teeming with delicious fish, such as tuna, bonito and wrass. The Tahitians lacked both clay and metal for pots and pans. The solution they found to the problem of preparing food without them was ingenious indeed. They baked it in an earth oven. This was simply a hole in the ground lined with boulder stones which they heated by making a fire on them. The food was carefully wrapped in leaves, placed on the hot stones and covered with earth. An hour later they would open the oven and take out the food. It would be baked, full of flavor, and wonderfully juicy and tender.

In a country with such a warm, even climate as Tahiti, the need for protective clothing was of course slight. For some reason the Polynesian peoples were ignorant of the arts of spinning and weaving, and the Tahitians, like their neighbors in nearby islands, made their clothes and bed sheets from the soft inner bark of the mulberry, the breadfruit and the banyan trees, by glueing and beating strips together until a rectangular piece of the same texture as thick paper was produced. It required only a

to examine here to what extent, if at all, this firm and widespread belief in the Tahitian paradise is justified. We must of course clearly distinguish between the past and the present, for in Tahiti, as elsewhere in the world, the changes have been tremendous since the first white men landed here more than 200 years ago.

These were, in Tahiti, English and French sailors who made up the crews of navy ships dispatched to the Pacific to make new discoveries and conquests. Lieutenant Samuel Wallis RN won by a narrow margin when, during an otherwise uneventful circumnavigation of the globe, he sighted Tahiti in June 1769. It was nine months before his French rival, Capitaine Louis-Antoine de Bougainville, cast anchor. As Bougainville was unaware of Wallis' discovery we can, if we want to be charitable to the French, accept their frequently repeated claim that Tahiti is in the unique position of having been discovered independently by two different navigators. The accounts left by Wallis and Bougainville are very sketchy. Fortunately for us, another navigator of a much greater genius, energy and curiosity, the immortal Captain Cook, came to Tahiti four times during his three great voyages of exploration in the Pacific, and he has

Tahitian families like this
one in Papeete have produced
numerous children — and a
population of which
55 per cent are under 20.

A Maupiti islander grates
coconut flesh to make milk.
Her house is built in the
traditional manner of palm
thatched bamboo canes.

Tahitians Polynesia

The volcanic island of
Bora Bora, north-west of
Tahiti, rises steeply from
the peaceful waters of
its surrounding lagoon.

It is possibly Gauguin's view of the sensuous, mysterious Tahitian beauty that brings the flocks of visitors: the mystery may now elude them.

Compared to the harsh life they left in England, Tahiti seemed an earthly paradise to the 18th century English sailors, its first visitors.

little more effort to build a house of the traditional Tahitian type, with walls of bamboo canes and a roof of plaited pandanus or coconut leaves. All the men in the village helped in the building of each such hut and they usually lasted from five to ten years.

Since the same foods and goods could be and were produced by all the households, and the inhabitants of the surrounding islands had nothing else or better to offer, there was no reason to barter or trade. This left the Tahitians plenty of leisure which they used in a pleasurable way. Their favorite pastimes were singing, dancing and playing games. Of the games only boxing and wrestling were of a moderately violent character, and the most popular ones were such peaceful amusements as stilt walking, kite flying, arrow shooting and surfing, the last one of course being the most typical of all the local sports in Polynesia.

The impression retained by the earliest European visitors who came to Tahiti, of a simple, innocent people living close to nature, was reinforced by the vigor and health of the islanders. Their bodies were strong and harmoniously built, their teeth perfect and ivory white. The only drink they knew was the fresh, cool river water which flowed down from the high mountains in the interior of the island. Thanks to this abundance of fresh water they could, and did, bath several times a day. Also the isolated position of Tahiti, so far from the surrounding continents, had prevented the diseases that killed, plagued and disfigured a large portion of humanity from reaching the shores of this happy island. They were a healthy as well as a happy people.

It is fairly easy to observe accurately such things as the way people eat and dress and all the external aspects of their lives. The accounts left by the earliest visitors to Tahiti of these material manifestations of the island culture are therefore, as a rule, reliable. But to understand and record the family life, the system of government and the religious beliefs of a newly discovered people requires a complete mastery of their language, and it was precisely this knowledge that Wallis, Bougainville and Cook lacked. Misled by the simple agriculture, rudimentary technology and the few material possessions of the Tahitians, they concluded quite understandably, but erroneously, that these happy children of nature had no laws, no institutions, no constraints and no moral laws. They concluded that the Tahitians were guided purely by their instincts, and had realized an ideal society which was based on complete fraternity, equality and liberty. It is an ideal that has always been the rosy dream of mankind.

Nothing could have been more wrong. Tahitian society was in fact extremely aristocratic. A ruling caste of hereditary chiefs lorded it over a mass of commoners who could never rise above the class barriers. This does not imply that there was oppression or exploitation. The facts tend to prove that the situation was much worse for 79 a commoner in Europe during the 18th century, when Tahiti was discovered. But if the Tahitians had been able to read all the nonsense their European admirers wrote about their free, natural life, they certainly would have laughed. They would have found the observations and comments on their sexual customs particularly amusing. There were definitely fewer sexual rules than in Europe. They permitted complete premarital and a certain amount of extramarital intercourse with clearly designated persons. But there was no general promiscuity. This would have brought about chaos, and no people in history has managed to survive such a complete license.

Their religion was lofty and complex, and the Tahitians worshipped numerous gods with many sacrifices, lengthy prayers and intricate ritual. As to the feeling of fraternity which, it was alleged, pervaded Tahitian social and political life, in fact the various tribes in Tahiti were often at war with each other. Or I should perhaps rather use the word skirmish instead of war to avoid any suspicion that the Tahitians were capable of the same systematic, prolonged cruelties as the governments and armies of our modern, so called civilized, states. In accordance with the prevailing spirit of chivalry of the Tahitians, many of the battles were fought in the form

of single combats, and the only arms the warriors possessed were wooden spears, clubs and stone slings.

For a people so ill-equipped for their defense as the Tahitians were, the introduction of firearms brought immediate disaster. Those responsible for this crime were sailors, lured by the prospect of an indolent and voluptuous life, who deserted ships and settled among the Tahitians, often taking the daughter of some ambitious chief for 'wife'. At the same time they began to sell liquor and to teach the islanders how to distil. The greatest number of these ruffians and beachcombers arrived not on the navy ships, whose captains were strict disciplinarians, but on the American and English whaling vessels that used the Pacific as their principal hunting ground during the first half of the 19th century. The only other white men to settle in Tahiti during this period were missionaries, the first of whom represented the London Missionary Society, a non-conformist organization. French Catholic missionaries followed around 1840 and the ensuing conflict resulted eventually in a French take-over. Tahiti and the surrounding islands remain today an overseas territory of France called French Polynesia.

A trip round the island reveals to what extent all these

Canoes with a long outrigger boom attached for stability, like this one sailing in Tahaa lagoon, are found throughout the Pacific.

By night as well as by day
Tahitians sail the lagoons
in search of fish. Attracted
by the light, the fish are
lured into the nets.

sea captains, sailors, missionaries, traders and colonial
servants have succeeded in civilizing, or rather westerniz-
ing the Tahitians. The task is easy. There is an excellent
sealed road which completely encircles the main island
(whose circumference is barely 80 miles) and most of the
smaller peninsula. This road runs everywhere next to
the beach, and immediately beyond this narrow coastal
strip the mountains rise steeply to two summits, more
than 2,000 feet high. The whole interior of the island
presents such a chaos of ravines, chasms and rugged
hills that no human habitation or even penetration
is possible.

Outside the overgrown capital of Papeete the prevailing impression everywhere in and around the small
clusters of houses that dot the landscape, is one of pro-

Tahitians have adapted the
western sport of horse racing
and added it to their ancient
pastimes: boxing, wrestling,
kite flying and surfing.

Women and children join the men helping to hold up a large seine net for a gigantic catch in Bora Bora Lagoon.

The Tahitians themselves do not eat beef, but several thousand beef and dairy cattle are kept on the island for the hotel trade.

82

found peace. The men and women sit quietly and chat on their verandas or work at a leisurely pace in their flower-filled gardens, with the children playing and splashing in the rivers. If a warrior can be found today, he is one of the many hundred Tahitian veterans who fought voluntarily and valiantly in Europe in World War I and World War II for the mother country, the French Republic.

Though the number of stores has greatly increased since the whaling days, only a few are owned or managed by Tahitians. To do business and haggle is still below their dignity and besides, they find it boring to spend their life indoors behind a counter. In their place, in the small shops and stores as well as in the new supermarkets that line the road, we find, of course, sometimes the descendants of sailors who once deserted a whaling

liquor, beer and wine, but others are sober-minded enough to invest their money in wiser ways. Today many of the descendants of the native Tahitians discovered by Wallis and Bougainville are dressed in European clothes, and own British-style bungalows built of imported Oregon pine and corrugated iron. They buy corned beef, bread, coffee and sugar, which they prepare on a petrol stove, rather than go through the old laborious process of cooking in an earth oven.

There are 18 rural districts in Tahiti, and in each one the spire of a Protestant church rises above the palm trees. The pastors are not British or French any longer but native Tahitians, as a result of the autonomy the Metropolitan Evangelical Church gave its former mission in 1963. In half of the districts a Catholic, and quite often a Mormon or an Adventist, Church can also be found. It is an undisputed fact that the missionaries and the pastors have done much good for the Tahitians, as teachers and unselfish guides to the strange ways of the white men. But at the same time, the mere existence of so many competing churches and faiths, each claiming to be the only true one, has sown confusion and doubts in the minds of the Tahitians.

Finally in every district there are imposing and enduring monuments to the glory of the new rule brought by the French in the form of two ugly concrete buildings. The first one is the *Mairie*, or Town Hall, where the democratically elected mayor carries out his light duties, mostly confined to the registration of births, marriages and deaths. The second official building is the primary school, where the children can be seen through the perpetually open windows more or less eagerly copying irregular French verbs or reciting some fables by La Fontaine. During the recreations the school yard is full of children playing volley ball, marbles or hop-scotch.

When one sees the great number of children – 55 per cent of the population of 80,000 is below 20 years of age – the important question arises immediately whether and how they will be able to make a living when they grow up. The answer is to be found along the coastal road, for as we approach Papeete again several huge hotels occasionally block the view of the lagoon. Tourism is the solution to all present and future economic problems that the government has adopted. So far the number of tourists has steadily increased from year to year and there is every reason to believe that they will keep coming in larger and larger droves.

With more Tahitians working in the hotels and restaurants everybody will have more money, and will of course use it to buy more European food, clothes, gadgets and cars. And at the same time the development of the tourist industry will tend to preserve certain aspects of the ancient culture, such as the dances, the songs and the music. For these are all part of the myth of the earthly paradise that the visitors expect and therefore must always find in Tahiti.

vessel or the descendants of colonial servants who stayed for good during the last century. But most of the shopkeepers and businessmen are Chinese, the children or grand-children of poor coolies who arrived via the goldfields in Ballarat and Klondike. Industriously putting all their children and relatives to work, they have long since completely monopolized the retail trade.

The Tahitians who have wanted to earn money have hitherto either chosen to make copra from the coconuts that grow on their family lands, or they have turned to the sea and become professional fishermen, going out to sea 40 or 50 miles to catch tuna, bonito and sword-fish. And during the last few years they have begun to work in ever greater numbers in town as dockers, masons, carpenters and truck drivers. Many of them are still inclined to spend their earnings on large quantities of hard

83

Fijians
Melanesia

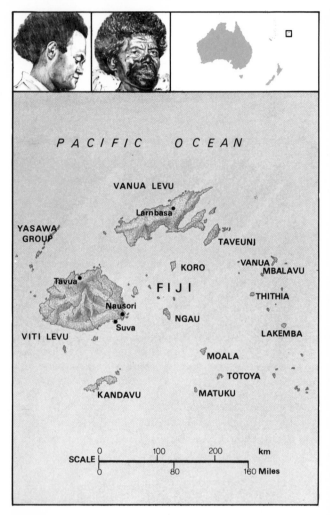

PACIFIC OCEAN

VANUA LEVU

Larnbasa

YASAWA GROUP

TAVEUNI

KORO

VANUA MBALAVU

Tavua

FIJI

THITHIA

Nausori

NGAU

Suva

VITI LEVU

LAKEMBA

MOALA

TOTOYA

KANDAVU

MATUKU

SCALE 0 100 200 km
0 80 160 Miles

Captain Bligh, set adrift in a dinghy after the mutiny of *HMS Bounty* accidentally discovered the Fiji group of islands in 1789. For a time they were known as Bligh's Islands. In a less painful fashion Tasman, Cook, Wilson and von Bellinghausen discovered odd islands in the group, without realizing either the vast extent of the Fiji archipelago – the largest in the Pacific – or its extraordinary cultural diversity.

Some of Fiji's islands are coral atolls that just peep above the water. Others are volcanic mountains 4,000 feet high with lagoons down below edged by coral reefs. Over the ages the heavy rainfall has carved out unexpectedly wide, long rivers. The landscape ranges from densest jungle to sparse savanna. The principal means of transport is, as ever, boats of every shape and size, but now roads reach once-remote villages, there is a local air service, and there is a sugar company railway which carries passengers free along a narrow gauge across road-bridges shared by automobiles. There are pandanus fruit, and beckoning you on around every twist and turn of the road the heady fragrance of frangipani and

Essential ingredients of
Fijian life are decorum,
friendliness, and kava
(fermented from peppers) here
quaffed by a fisherman.

At the kava ceremony, performed at any important meeting, a servant tests the drink for poison, then offers it to the guest of honor.

(Bottom) These sugar cane fields give Fiji its main income. Indians were imported as labor, but indigenous Fijians now grow sugar too.

(Right) Many Fijians are fire-walkers. They walk sharply — but they never run — across stones heated beforehand till white hot.

gardenia. The casuarina, Tahitian chestnut and barringtonia trees rise up in unforgettably bizarre postures.

Of the few animals on Fiji, wild pigs, which often ferociously attack men and dogs out hunting, are the most dangerous. There are countless bats – eaten by some tribes and revered by others – rats and giant toads. Insects are the most troublesome form of animal life on the islands. Mosquitoes, although not malarial, carry elephantiasis and dengue fever. Flies, giant flying cockroaches and ants have to be kept away from food. Vicious centipedes lurk in latrines.

In the sea there are not only hordes of ferocious sharks, but the even fiercer barracuda. Giant stingrays leap vertically high out of the water, then descend with a heavy sharp smack back into the ocean. The black and white banded and goldheaded sea-snakes insinuate, beautiful and sinister through the clear water. Whales, whose teeth the Fijians prize and present as symbols of welcome, warily stay out in the distant deeps, but turtles are not adroit enough to avoid being eagerly captured by the islanders. Their heads make a final appearance proudly placed on the chief's plate.

On the outer reefs men spear kingfish, swordfish, tuna and octopus. At night they put out to sea with lanterns in punts and canoes and take heavy catches often made

A patient Fijian prepares
coconuts for copra, an
important export. He leaves
them in the sun and the
flesh curls away from the shell.

Queen Elizabeth's portrait tops this collection of pictures, some on loan — and by the custom of *kerekere* they need not be returned.

heavier by the fish who jump into the craft. If you are awakened early next morning by a blast of the conch shell you know that the catch has been so big that the fishermen have more than enough for themselves, enough to sell. In the lagoons goggled women stay immersed for hours netting prawns, crabs and mullet and collecting fish trapped in fences. Land crabs taste good but giant coconut-crabs are an acquired taste, for the gourmet only. Although fish are relatively scarce along the rivers even 20-30 miles upstream Fijians with old tins scoop out delectable whitebait in thousands.

The people who followed the explorers to Fiji were traders in pursuit of sandalwood and bêche-de-mer (sea slugs). Then came missionaries. The earliest European beachcombers brought their knowledge of firearms to Fiji and the islands soon became so wracked by inter-tribal warfare that they were in danger of being taken over by the able Tongan prince Ma'afu'otu'itonga who already controlled the more Polynesian half of the archipelago. In 1874 the chiefs under Bau Island's paramount leader Ratu Ebenezer Seru Cakoban – who had a

shaky claim to the title of King of Fiji – decided that only strong government could save Fiji, so they gave Fiji to Queen Victoria. Almost one hundred years later, in 1970, Britain gave Fiji back to the Fijians, culturally remarkably intact.

The relationship between Britain and Fiji has always been one of respect and goodwill. Britain had neither bought nor conquered the islands. There was a policy of understanding between European District Commissioners and Fijian chiefs, of preserving many Fijian customs and laws, and of insisting that Fijians should never be deprived of their own land. Today the descendants of the chiefs retain the self-respect and power of their ancestors.

The special language for talking to chiefs is still spoken. And there remain some objects which are for chiefs alone. Only the son of a chief's sister may take any of the chief's possessions, and often does. Chief's possessions are never subject to *kerekere* by which any Fijian may borrow any article which he desires, without the duty to give it back. These objects include white ornamental cowrie shells which denote aristocratic canoes, house-posts, *yaqona* bowls, and neckbands. As no Fijian except chiefs can refuse such a request, it is hardly surprising that Fijians who try to keep stores usually go bankrupt. Storekeeping is sadly incompatible with *kerekere*. This may explain why successful stores in Fiji are run by Indians or Chinese.

Fiji is at the crossroads of Pacific sea-traffic. Suva, its capital, is the busiest center in the South Pacific. The Fijians produce copra, gold, bananas and ginger, and they import flour, meat, fish, machinery, petrol, textiles and vehicles. Their main source of income is sugar cane, cultivated originally by specially imported Indian indentured laborers, as Fijians themselves refused to do the work. Indians now outnumber indigenous Fijians on the islands.

The cash and consumer economy has come to Fiji in a big way. Co-existing as incongruously with the cash economy as *kerekere*, the unsolicited appropriation of another man's goods, is the economic custom of *solevu*. By this system, articles made in one region are exchanged with a different type of article made in another. Unlike *kerekere, solevu* has great economic and practical advantages. It encourages Fijians to keep up the particular skills of their region. In some communities, fishermen and craftsmen are not only specialists, but clans apart. Indeed craftsmen would not be regarded as members of the community: they would be denied membership even by marriage and would not be allowed to own land, but would be looked after by the high chief himself. Under the chief's protection they make clubs, spears, wooden pillows, combs, *lali* (gongs), canoes, house posts, and along with the Maori are the best carpenters in all the south Pacific. Women make clay-sand pots, bark cloth (tapa), and weave jute used to make fans and as a building material for houses. In the village the houses and thatched kitchens are sparsely furnished: a simple upright chair, the plainest of tables, a meat-safe with its legs in meat tins full of water to drown ants, a few cooking utensils, clothes, sometimes a mosquito-net, mats, the odd family photograph, pictures of the British royal family: there is not much else. Fijians have little interest in material possessions.

In each village there are 20 to 1,000 inhabitants, made up of family units. Land is owned through kinship (or *tokatoka*). When a man dies his wealth passes to his brothers, who on their death leave it to their eldest sons. Although it is usually the primary aim of each family in a village just to subsist, pressure on simple villagers to act for the wider public good comes all the way down to them from the top. Every villager in every village is expected to contribute to the community or village. Sometimes villages will combine to jointly carry out the special request of an important chief to whom all owe allegiance. For an occasion like the marriage of the paramount chief's daughter, for example, each village would take on specific duties: one village might make tapa; one would provide firewood for the ovens in which pigs laid on by another village and turtles, caught by another would be cooked; one village might bring scented coconut-oil, another yams, or tapioca. Only occasionally does a village complain that its task is too heavy, for it is usually outweighed by family loyalties and the universal Fijian delight in team-work. As a reward the change of scene and activity, the dancing, *yaqona* drinking, feasting and socializing more than compensate for the hard work.

Village relationships are not, however, always so co-operative. By the custom of *veitauvu* two villages from different federations are haphazardly paired by virtue of sharing an ancestral god. In Lau in the far east of Fiji, a village could be *veitauvu* with another in the extreme west. The custom confers on either village the dubious right not only to take any goods it fancies from the other but also to treat it rudely and harshly.

However badly a village is abused by the village with which it is so arbitrarily *veitauvu* it must take its treatment with a smile. Once when I was driving along with a Fijian magistrate whose own province was on the other side of the main island I offered a Fijian woman a lift just outside her village. I had expected her just to hop in the back. But my fellow magistrate insisted, before she got in, that as he and she were *veitauvu* he would have to go and sit in the back. This was doubly unusual because as she was female and of inferior rank the back of the car was undoubtedly her proper place. But from the back of the car she would have been entitled to exercise her *veitauvu* right to pummel the back of his head with her fists and beat it with her basket. In no other circumstances may the Fijian head even be touched.

On another occasion in the Viti Levu highlands, my

(Top) At the funeral of the Chief of Lauam, tapa mats from all over Fiji and Tonga were placed on the ground for mourners to sit on.

The tranquillity of this moment of remembrance reflects careful planning and the Fijians' deep sense of community cooperation.

Mourners may not weep till
the body has been buried.
Instead, the air fills
with the sound of conch
shells being blown.

The Lauam chief's coffin,
draped with the British
Union Jack, is carried slowly
to the burial ground by men
of Fiji's highest families.

matanovanua, who traveled everywhere with me as my
herald, mouthpiece and right-hand man for ceremonial
protocol, and who came from a Lauan island, was
sitting quietly inside a thatched house after an official
welcoming ceremony from which women were excluded.
Suddenly half-a-dozen women crept in and set on him,
belaboring his head with bamboo chunks. He fled from
the hut but they chased him and he only escaped by
swimming across the river in complete darkness. Next
morning when he had joined me in the put-put (a punt
with an engine making a put-put noise) the women
suddenly re-appeared, set upon him, toppled him out
into the river and poured mud all over him.

Fijians have kept intact most of their old customs,
although missionaries and the British government did
suppress some of them. Cannibalism, for example, is
one practice that fifty years of missionary propaganda
and courage did end. Fijians were once possibly the   91

Fijians Melanesia

world's most voracious cannibals. Perhaps the Fijians were only able to survive their long voyages of emigration on human food. Possibly there were no edible animals on the islands. Or perhaps devouring the vanquished endowed the victor with spiritual strength.

But the missionaries certainly did not destroy totems and taboos which continue to flourish, particularly in the highlands. A Fijian of any status who absent-mindedly plucks a forbidden flower for example, or casually mentions a certain species of bird, is liable to be assaulted or thrown by women into the nearest water.

At almost every special occasion – like the welcome of an official or chief – Fijians present a whale's tooth which is received with thanks in a time-honored formula, the kava ceremony, which usually only men attend. To historic chants punctuated with complete silence the welcomers mix the kava with serious ritual and impressive dignity. They offer it to the chief guest, then to his *matanivanua*, to the next guest and his *matanivanua*, to the local chief and his *matanivanua*, and so on. The welcome ceremony closes with dances by men, women or by both in succession but not together.

If a high official arrives at a Lauan island by sea, a party puts out to sea a great line with a whale's tooth – an invitation to pull up anchor and approach the coast. With another tooth they invite him to wade ashore. On land the welcomers solemnly offer him a strip of coconut matting to represent the dry earth upon which he has landed after his oceanic wanderings, a stalk bearing two green coconuts to epitomize an offering of the fruits of the soil, and a root of the chief's *yaqona* plant. They then present him with another whale's tooth, which means 'please lower your war pennant.' Next they present him with tapa – an offer to change into dry clothing. Finally, they mix *yaqona*, which the high-ranking guest from over the sea must drink with his hosts. Few Europeans have been accorded this privilege. On Lau where Fijian ceremonial is at its most polished, at Christmas or New Year spirits and temperature are high and the celebrations are less formal, more intimate. On these occasions Lauan women are likely to pour scented coconut oil and talcum powder over a male guest's head, an uncomfortable mark of their affection.

In fact there is a diversity of customs on Fiji that

92

Swimming fish-drivers, always fully clothed, encircle their prey, which they trap and spear. This woman bites her prey dead.

reflects their diversity of race. Seated on a bench in Suva it can be challenging to guess the racial origins of the passers-by. Fijians are possibly only really alike in one respect, their courtesy. Lauans, for example, who live half-way between Fiji and Tonga, are easily distinguishable from Fijians from the mountains, plains and villages of Colo, the interior of Viti Levu. Their complexion is paler, and they seem more self-assured. On Vanuabalavu, there is the Tongan village of Sawana. Here Tongan is taught by Tongan teachers; the church is Tongan in character; and their ceremony of welcome is Tongan: just like the Tongan monarch, the chief guest is given the third cup of kava after two heralds (one for the hosts and one for the guest) have tasted the first two for poison. Then there is the Rotuman Group, a dependency of Fiji discovered when *HMS Bounty's* mutineers were being sought, which was offered to Britain in 1881. Some 200 miles north of Fiji the language and customs veer towards Polynesian and Micronesian. The Rotumans' origins remain mysterious – the people may have Mongolian and European strains. There are the former inhabitants of Ocean Island, the Banabans, who were transferred to a Fijian island after the Japanese had overrun their homes. And Ellice Islanders (Polynesians) from Vaitupu, who bought a neighboring island in Fiji.

Most of Fiji's quarter of a million Indians are Hindus, descendants of those who opted to stay after their indentures expired. (After 1916 no more Indian plantation workers were allowed in.) They are a little more adaptable to Fiji conditions than the more rigid Muslim minority. Many of the Indian community now grow sugar or rice on land which they lease from Fijians. Some work for the sugar company. In some towns nearly all stores are owned by Gujaratis. The Indians are sufficiently untouched by their Fijian surroundings to adhere to their special customs in marriage, death, and religion. Fire-walking as displayed by the south Indians is quite different from, and more impressive than, the feat of the Fijian Beqa islanders, who walk on a special hot surface. The Indians have multiplied more quickly than Fijians who, although they learned to resist diseases like tuberculosis, increase more slowly. The Indians already outnumbered the indigenous Fijians by the end of World War II.

There are versatile part-Europeans in all parts of Fiji – many of them working in managerial capacities, in government departments, in the sugar industry and running copra plantations. Fiji's bankers are Chinese who are otherwise mainly store-keepers. Not the best linguists, they speak Cantonese among themselves and find it equally hard to express themselves in Fijian, Hindi and English.

Although Fiji is a harmonious multi-racial society in which people of every type and origin work well together there are areas of racial exclusiveness. People who work together do not necessarily play together. Many Euro-

peans for example, have resisted lowering social barriers which, especially since Fijian independence in 1970, must slowly crumble. People tend to enjoy their leisure among friends of their own race. Religious differences (Fijians are themselves about 90 per cent Wesleyan) and broadcasts in the different vernaculars have emphasized sectarianism. Sport brings people together, but only to a limited extent. Table tennis brought the Chinese into Fijian social life, but Fijians themselves prefer Rugby football. Indians play cricket, hockey and football.

Although Fijians are highly intelligent and reasonably literate, they have never shown the same competitiveness or ambition as Europeans. Unlike the Indians they have never regarded it as overwhelmingly important to educate their offspring. It does not seem generally to occur to Fijians that by doing so their children would become the future doctors, lawyers and engineers of Fiji. For the extrovert, friendly, generous Fijians, who one hundred years ago preferred to entrust their islands to the government of a distant island on the other side of the world rather than see them decimated by bloody war, it is enough to live together in amicable peace.

Indians now outnumber indigenous Fijians. In a religious conversion ceremony men drive silver skewers into their bodies.

93

Easter islanders
Polynesia

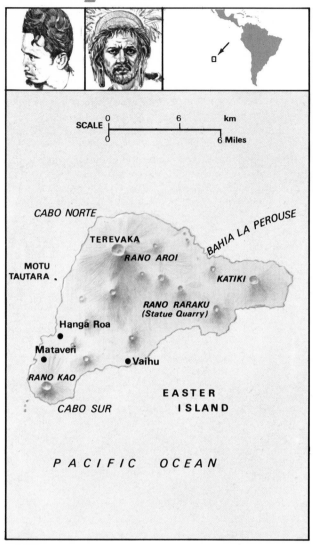

On Easter Day in 1722, the Dutch admiral Jacob Roggeveen, sailing west across the Pacific, ran into an unknown island half-way between South America and the nearest islands of south-eastern Polynesia. He named his discovery Easter Island, unaware of the name the stone age people who received him ashore already had for, their most isolated of all human settlements – *Te-Pito-o-te-Henua* or 'the navel of the world'. The barren island, measuring only seven by fourteen miles, was surrounded by nearly 2,000 miles of open ocean in all directions.

Dotting the bare landscape were hundreds of colossal stone giants. These gave rise to one of the major archaeological mysteries of the world. Even today, past and present are so completely mingled on this tiny island that it is impossible to understand one without considering the other. In spite of the recent introduction of Christianity and modern continental culture, the Easter

A lone horseman is dwarfed
by the mysterious 30 foot
statues erected long ago by
his ancestors' foes, the Long
Ears, probably from Peru.

A family takes a stroll after mass. A permanent Christian mission was set up only in 1934 and ancient superstitions still have a strong hold.

The largest of these stone giants weighs 82 tons. Erected as monuments to long-dead chieftains, they stare out across 2,000 miles of ocean.

islanders live in the shadow of their ancestral enterprises.

The Dutch discoverers were the first to see the Easter islanders in their aboriginal state, and they found a population that evidently contained various ethnic strains. Whereas some were dark and black-haired, there were others among them as white as Europeans, with blond hair and beards, and still others of a reddish tint as if they had been burnt by the sun. After the single day's visit by the Dutch, Easter Island received no further visits until it was rediscovered by the Spaniards from Peru in 1770. Again the islanders were described as a mixed population. Many, the Spaniards observed, had red or cinnamon-colored hair. Many of the men were of great stature, and two, measured by the Spaniards out of curiosity, were found to be 6 feet 5 inches and 6 feet 6½ inches tall. The last of a series of civil wars, however, ravaged the island and sharply reduced the number of people in the four year period prior to Captain James Cook's visit in 1774. By the time Cook arrived there were very few people left; the women were represented merely by a handful of old crones. He described the islanders he did see as small, lean and miserable, and of obvious Polynesian stock. Whereas the earliest visitors had received great quantities of American sweet potatoes and chili peppers as well as Polynesian bananas and chickens, the condition of the islanders was now so distressed that they were unable to part with adequate provisions for Captain Cook's crew.

In 1862, after a few more visits from Europeans, many of the island people were carried away to Peru as slaves. When repatriated, the slaves brought a small-pox epidemic to the island which in 1877 reduced the population to no more than 111. In 1864 Brother Eugène Eyraud settled on the island and did his best to alleviate the misery; but the islanders stole from him mercilessly. He left on the next ship. Returning two years later with three other missionaries, he and his followers were once more driven from the island even though the islanders had officially been converted to Christianity. A permanent

From these rocks islanders watch for the arrival of migrating birds. The first man to find an egg becomes Bird Man, a semi-god for the year.

A statue of the Virgin of Rapanui stands in the island's church. Wood carving has replaced farming as the islanders' main income.

97

Easter islanders Polynesia

Increased contact with Chile
has enabled the islanders to
replace the old reed huts
with pre-fabricated houses,
a hospital and a school.

A dinghy and outboard motor
have replaced the boats made
of reeds brought from Peru
and planted in island
lakes by ancient settlers.

Islanders still believe
aku-aku or ancestral spirits
hold power at Ahu-Hanga-Tee,
a burial place dating
from the 17th century.

mission was not established on the island until the arrival of Father Sebastian Englert in 1934.

After the Chilean annexation of the island in 1888, a naval vessel began calling at two or three year intervals. Until recently these visits became established as a regular annual event. Since 1967 tourism has increased, an airport for trans-Pacific traffic has been opened, and the islanders are now fully exposed to continental culture.

Until a few years ago, almost the entire island was leased to sheep farmers and the aboriginal population confined to a restricted area on the west coast around the only settlement, Hangaroa village. With no outside supplies except those brought on the brief yearly visit of the Chilean warship, the islanders sustained themselves by coastal fishing and primitive agriculture, growing mainly the traditional sweet potato. But increased contact with Chile—involving the building of a school, hospital and stores—has rapidly changed the islanders' way of life. The population has grown to about 1,200, almost all of whom are natives, rather than settlers on the island. Until a few years ago, the island had the highest percentage of leprosy in the world, but the inmates of the local leper colony have now dropped from more than 10 per cent of the island population to less than 1 per cent.

The youngest Easter Island generation includes few, if any, of pure island blood, although many of the older people claim direct descent from one or the other of the two local traditional tribes, the Long-Ears and the Short-Ears, which shared the island in pre-European times. The Long-Ears earned their name because of their custom of extending their earlobes, as can be seen on the large stone statues and wooden figurines of the island. According to traditions which survived the arrival of the first Europeans two different culture heroes, *Hotu Matua* and *Tuu-Ko-iho,* had brought immigrants to the island from opposite directions. The legends claim that *Hotu Matua* and the Long-Ears had come on a 60-day voyage from the direction of the sunrise – from the east, from South America. They came from a desert land called the 'burial place' where 'the climate was so intensely hot that the people sometimes died from the effects of the heat, and at certain seasons, plants and growing things were shriveled up by the burning sun'.

Westward from Easter Island, all the way to southeast Asia, there is no land that corresponds to this description. In this direction the islands have not arid but verdant coasts, often covered in dense jungle. But to the east, as legend recalls, lying 60 days distant, there is the desert coast of Peru. All along this coast there are abundant necropolises, many of which grew to fill vast areas, accumulating human remains and funeral objects. In fact, the desert climate with the burial grounds provide modern anthropologists and archaeologists with much evidence which can be used either to counter or to support the recollections of legend.

The legends say that *Tuu-Ko-iho* and the Short-Ears, on 99

Wheat flour brought by sea from Chile means that this bakery can provide fresh bread each day.

(Bottom) Since 1967 and the building of an airport, tourism has become one of Easter Island's main hopes for the future.

Visits from Chilean naval vessels are an important annual event. Young islanders welcome the navy's school ship with a traditional dance.

the other hand, came from the west, from the direction of Polynesia, and that they arrived 30 generations after *Hotu Matua*. The Short-Ears adopted the customs and beliefs of the Long-Ears and for two centuries the two peoples lived in peace. They were also jointly responsible for the monuments which dominate the Easter Island landscape. For the Short-Ears helped the Long-Ears in their great stone works. Twelve generations before the arrival of the missionaries on the island there was a rebellion: the Short-Ears had grown tired of toiling for the Long-Ears. A battle followed in which the Long-Ears were defeated. They were burnt in a defensive pyre in a deep ditch they had built across a cliff-girt peninsula on the eastern tip of Easter Island. Modern excavations have been able to prove the existence of the legendary pyre and carbon dating has shown that it burnt roughly 300 years before our own time.

But how do these legends correspond with historical and archaeological observations? The Dutch had observed the remarkable differences between many of the Easter islanders. From their observations that some were almost white, with fair hair and others dark, with black hair came the assumptions that Easter Island had been visited and settled by fair-skinned people unlike those found elsewhere in Polynesia (like the Short-Ears) or

people in South America. Many early 20th century writers argued that there was ample evidence that Easter Island had been originally settled by migrants from Egypt or Mesopotamia. There were obvious parallels between the culture of the Old World and that of Easter Island: fitted megalithic masonry, stepped temple pyramids, monolithic statues, gods of solar lineage, hieroglyphic tablets.

In Peru, on the western desert coast of South America, there were (and are) legends which tell of white, bearded migrants who first appeared from an unspecified region and departed into the Pacific long before the Spaniards arrived. And when the Spaniards came they found in Peru some members of the local ruling classes who were 'whiter than Spaniards' and others who had fair hair. In the well-preserved tombs of the desert coast, this evidence of diverse physical character was confirmed. Many of the mummies had fair hair and a facial structure closer to the European type than to the Indian which is round and Asiatic. Here, perhaps, was evidence of Easter Island's Long-Ears.

In ancient Egypt, the Sun and the Sun God were known and worshipped as *Ra*; and on all the hundreds of islands of Polynesia, *Ra* was again the name of the sun. Polynesian traditions speak of *Uru* as an important tribal and place name in the homeland of their ancestors; this has often been interpreted as a reference to the ancient Mesopotamian culture center of *Ur*, but it is also the name of an ancient tribe from Peru's Lake Titicaca. This tribe is assumed to have formerly dominated the entire area from the megalithic ruins of Tiahuanaco down to the Pacific coast. At the time of the Spanish Conquest, the *Uru* were the principal builders of reed-boats on the lake and they lived on floating islands of Totora reed. This same reed had been brought by man to Easter Island and planted in lakes for the very purpose of building reed-boats like those used on Lake Titicaca.

The feasibility of a voyage from the coast of Peru to Easter Island was demonstrated in 1947 when the balsa raft *Kon Tiki* sailed and drifted along the Mendaña ocean current between South America and Polynesia. Although at sea for more than 100 days, the raft became neither waterlogged, nor impossible to navigate. It is hardly in doubt that pre-Columbian navigators from South America could have completed the voyage with as much ease. Since 1947 seven other raft voyages from Peru to the Pacific islands have been successfully accomplished. A totora reed boat has also sailed from Peru to Panama and the experiments with the reed boats Ra I and Ra II, of which the latter crossed the Atlantic, show that such vessels can sail even further than the distance from Peru to Easter Island. It seems likely that this was the means by which the inspiration for the great stone statues came to Easter Island; perhaps it is the answer to all the other remarkable parallels between ancient Peruvian culture and that of Easter Island.

The statues were monuments raised on temple platforms in honor of deceased kings and chiefs, some of whose names are still remembered and, as the generations passed on, larger and larger monuments were sculptured. The stone giants were first manoeuvered down the crater slopes, sliding on their unworked backs, and then tilted on end on a temporary foundation at the foot of the volcano. Here the sculptors were able to complete even the back before the reed-padded monument was dragged away on wooden skids to its final destination, which was one of the hundreds of large and often lofty stone platforms scattered about the island. The stone giants were erected on their final platforms by a system as ingenious as it was simple: with stout wooden levers, the monolith was jerked from side to side while an increasing cairn of stones was built under it, lifting it up and tilting it on to its base. Whereas the unfinished statues, half buried in silt at the foot of the quarries are all 'blind', those erected on their so called *ahu* platforms received deep eye sockets which were probably formerly inlaid like the smaller wooden figures of Easter Island and some of the small stone figurines. In addition to the eyes, the erected statues now also received a red stone *pukao* (topknot) to balance on top of the head.

The largest of the erected statues weighs 82 tons and the largest of the topknots weighs 30 tons. Erecting them involved the engineering skill of lifting the weight of six elephants on to a statue as high as a three or four storey building, with not even place for a foothold. At the time of tribal war all the *ahu* images were overthrown, and until several were re-erected in recent years the only standing statues were the blind and unfinished ones buried in silt at the foot of the quarries. These were believed to be of a different kind until modern excavations disclosed that they too are complete busts with long arms and fingers placed on the abdomen.

With the disastrous civil wars, all megalithic stonework ceased on Easter Island and all portable property was carried away and hidden in caves with concealed entrances. Theft has always been admired as a skill on Easter Island and heirlooms could only be protected by hiding them. At the time the missionaries arrived many of these heirlooms including small sculptures in wood and stone, as well as wooden tablets incised with the characters of a forgotten script (*rongo-rongo*), were observed in the native reed huts.

The volcanic island is honeycombed with both open and secret caves. Tempted by the high commercial value of ancestral aboriginal art, it is a pastime of many of the islanders to search for other families' secret storage caves. Although eager Christian churchgoers, the islanders are still extremely superstitious, and only the fear of *aku-aku* or ancestral spirits causes them to maintain the secrets of most of the caves which contain an endless variety of small and generally grotesque sculptures. Only a few of the wooden figurines and paraphernalia follow standard types, among them the emaciated goatee-bearded male, the flat, bearded woman; and the human figurine with a hook-beaked bird's head. As the original wooden specimens began to deteriorate in the caves, the modern population continued carving duplicates. This type of conventionalized wood carving is today the main source of income for the Easter islanders.

The Chilean government is now replanting trees on a large scale on the island which has been barren throughout historic times although pollen borings disclose that palms and other trees once covered the landscape before man completely destroyed them for agriculture and stone-work.

There is no running surface water on Easter Island, but in 1965 a pipe-line was built from the crater lake of Rano Kao to the village of Hangaroa. The modern population selects its own council headed by a mayor who represents the islanders to a locally residing governor. There is no sheltered port on the island and a landing can only be made by barge at a pier near Hangaroa village, or on the only major sandy beach, at Anakena bay on the north coast.

The island's future seems to depend to a great extent on the development of tourism and the success of the Chilean attempt to replace sheep ranging by replanting. 101

Pitcairn islanders
Polynesia

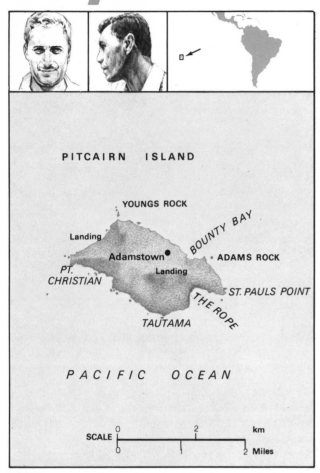

PITCAIRN ISLAND

YOUNGS ROCK

Landing

BOUNTY BAY

Adamstown

ADAMS ROCK

PT.
CHRISTIAN

Landing

ST. PAULS POINT

THE ROPE

TAUTAMA

PACIFIC OCEAN

SCALE 0 ... 2 ... km
0 ... 1 ... 2 Miles

The community on Pitcairn Island was truly founded in another place. Fletcher Christian, ship's mate of *HMS Bounty*, had taken enough insults from his commander William Bligh. Whether on impulse or after long deliberation, the crew led by Christian mutinied off the Tonga Islands in April 1789. They cast Bligh and those loyal to him adrift, and sailed off to Tahiti. It was the mutiny on the *Bounty* that started the Pitcairn community.

Relations between the Tahitians and the rebels soon deteriorated. Spurred on by the fear of discovery and arrest, nine mutineers led by Christian set off in search of an uninhabited island secure from the outside world. They brought with them twelve Polynesian women and six men.

For two months they combed the Cooks, Tonga and the eastern islands of Fiji in search of a home. Almost in desperation, Christian recalled or stumbled over an account by a Captain Carteret of an island in the far east of the Polynesian archipelago named after a young sailor in Carteret's crew called Pitcairn, the first to sight the island.

In early 1790 the *Bounty* had the good luck to reach it.

Explorers have found many relics of an ancient

103

Tiny Jackie Fletcher, like
most Pitcairners, is descended
from Tahitian women and
Fletcher Christian, leader of
HMS Bounty mutiny in 1789.

Pitcairn islanders Polynesia

Aged Ninette Christian sits outside Pitcairn Post Office, the colony's violent origins long ago forgotten. Her life has been tranquil.

Polynesian civilization on Pitcairn, but Carteret failed to make a landing and the mutineers must have thought they were the first men to live there. The mutineers and their Polynesian wives produced a number of children, but the Polynesian men fathered none. Almost everyone who lives on Pitcairn is descended from the children of the first mutineers and their Polynesian wives.

The early days of the settlement were turbulent. After ten years there was only one man alive, plus eight women and a number of children. The community suffered a dictatorship and two evacuations in the 19th century. Pitcairners have certainly had their ups and downs. But all in all they have achieved an astonishing harmony and a great love for their home. The Anglo-Polynesian people of Pitcairn have truly succeeded in turning a violent naval mutiny into a celebrated romance.

Pitcairn sits at the eastern tail-end of the scattered archipelagos of Polynesia. The nearest inhabited islands lie three hundred miles to the west. If you go south from Pitcairn the seas are empty till you come to the ice-caps of Antarctica. In its obscurity hidden halfway between

New Zealand and the Panama Canal, it is a tiny island only just over two miles long.

Yet to the intrepid mutineers and to anyone who approaches the island, it is daunting. It is so clumsy, so squat, its sides are so steep. Bounty Bay, where the islanders land their boats, is no real bay – it is barely a cove. Even on the calmest of days, heavy surf batters the coastline. From a distance the island looks like an upside-down canoe stuck firmly on a reef. As you get nearer you see the cliffs lift themselves almost sheer out of the sea to their full height, their reddish-black rock topped by bright white blotches – the islanders' houses. Nearer still, you realize the rich fertility of the place, the thick growth of lemon, orange and breadfruit trees whose generous covering softens the hard angles of the hills and cliffs and lends the island its feeling of heady luxuriance.

The mutineers anchored the *Bounty* in Bounty Bay and stripped her of all contents – pigs, chickens, yams and sweet potatoes as well as materials that could be used for building. They hauled them all up the steep and tricky Hill of Difficulty till they reached the Edge, a small grassy platform that overlooks the bay. Then they severed all links with the outer world: they ran the ship onto the rocky shore and burnt her.

Fletcher Christian was well-educated and a school-friend of the poet Wordsworth. He was mild, generous, sincere. Though the society he founded was essentially egalitarian, he was respected and looked up to as leader – his fellows always addressed him as 'Mr'. But he won their affection for his constant cheerfulness. His inner gloominess was reserved for the cave still known as Fletcher Christian's Cave. You can imagine him sitting up there in the cave mouth looking blankly out across the wastes of the Pacific, ruminating over a future career destroyed forever, going over the events that led to the mutiny and perhaps still gnawed by the anguish he had suffered. He died two years after the Pitcairn landing, but islanders remember him as the founder.

Four years after the mutiny only four men were left: Young, Adams, Quintal and McCoy. All the others had been killed through revolts by the women and the Polynesian men who had been brutally treated. Then the Scotsman McCoy learnt to brew a potent spirit in the ship's kettle. But his brew, made from the roots of the *ti* plant, drove him blindly and madly drunk, and he jumped over a cliff. Young died of asthma after he and Adams had axed to death the wild Cornish Quintal in self-defense. By 1800 Adams was the only man left.

Adams became the revered patriarch of his flock of ten Polynesian women and 23 children. He as much as Christian was the real founder of the community. He was a kindly man, a Cockney workshop orphan with but the roughest education. He could barely read, yet he taught the children from a prayerbook and the *Bounty's* bible now proudly preserved in the church. You can see

Pitcairners have twice tried to resettle elsewhere, but some came back, unable to live away from their minuscule, cosy island home.

Even the rough mutineers must have been daunted by the approach to the island. There is no good landing shore, let alone a harbor.

him in the mind's eye, laboriously decoding the words then forcefully impressing the truth of them upon his huge family. He maintained Christian's system of land-division, whereby the soil, originally cut into nine equal parts, one for each mutineer, fragmented into plots for the sailors' children. But above all, he was a stern Christian, fasting on Wednesday and Friday and holding prayer sessions at least once a day.

An American whaler discovered the community in 1808. In 1814 came the first British ship. It was not till 1825 that a British captain Beechey made a formal visit to the island, bringing with him a royal pardon for Adams. Real isolation had ended. The population multiplied. In 1831 the whole community was shipped to Tahiti for fear that Pitcairn could no longer hold so many people, but they were struck by disease and soon returned. Then they suffered under an upstart named Joshua Hill, who set himself up as their ruler and flogged the three islanders who dared to question his harsh and bigoted tyranny. He was possibly insane and certainly had ludicrous delusions of grandeur: his most extravagant claim was that he had once dined with Napoleon. He stayed for six years till 1838 when the islanders prevailed upon a passing British captain to free them. From this time the islanders considered themselves an official part of the British Empire, though the British passed an Act of Settlement over the island only in 1887.

In 1856 the islanders again evacuated the place but this time to an uninhabited land – Norfolk Island, which lies four thousand miles west. Norfolk is far larger than Pitcairn, but just as fertile. And with no people on it, there was no risk of disease. Most of the Pitcairners settled down happily, but homesickness for their original lonely isle went on nagging at a few. In 1858 two large families returned, joined by a further four in 1864. Altogether 43 people went back to the island they were not prepared to forsake. By 1937 the populace had swollen to 233, but by 1968 many of the young men,

105

Pitcairn islanders Polynesia

Though today's islanders have discarded their original Polynesian garb for European clothes, they still go barefoot like Tahitians.

Pitcairn sailors show their nautical prowess as their old-style longboat sweeps past menacing St Paul's Rock off the main island.

Here lies John Adams, a revered patriarch of the community, who was the only mutineer left 11 years after the mutiny. He died in 1829.

George III of England sent *HMS Bounty* to bring back the breadfruit tree. Nowadays mutineers' descendants make *Bounty* models out of it.

women tend to be a half-shade darker than the men. Hair is dark, with a suggestion of lighter color here and there. Many of them go barefoot, and you would notice that their feet are big. So are their hands – large, knobbly and calloused. They are large people, healthy and exceedingly strong. Their only widespread defect is their teeth, whose almost universal loss, especially among the older generation, has produced a curious sucking in of the cheeks and a collapse of the mouth. It is strange that observers have attributed a more English look to one sex and vice versa – but here lies the fascination that Pitcairn has for so many people. Certainly the mutiny and the success of founding a community on a deserted island is a romantic story. But to anthropologists, the study of hybrids has added interest. Most people throughout the world are in some way racially mixed, but the abruptness of the process on Pitcairn and the wide difference in looks and culture between the people thrown together in such odd circumstances make the Pitcairn islanders unique.

It is not surprising that with increased contact with the outer world Pitcairn should become predominantly European in culture. But it is strange that the process should have started right from the earliest days. And it is astonishing that when the island had only one English speaker on it – Adams – nevertheless English became the island's language.

Imagine the scene. Englishmen shouting at the Tahitian women – the traditional English way of impressing their language on foreigners; Tahitian women replying in elaborate gesticulations; a husband and a wife rearing a family but barely understanding each other. You would have thought, especially since mothers are the chief educators of the very young, that Tahitian would have become the Pitcairn language, the more so since from 1800 Adams was the sole English speaker, without even a companion to chat to and keep his mother tongue agile.

Today Pitcairners speak to strangers in a totally comprehensible and grammatical tongue, with a pleasant slurred drawl and musical rhythm that must be very far from the laborious grunts by which the first settlers communicated. The idiom is rather biblical due to strict religious upbringing based on the Bible; and rather nautical too – a clear heritage of Fletcher Christian and his fellows. And even when a Pitcairner is speaking his best, the stranger will be bewildered by geographical references that are bound to stud every Pitcairn conversation – like John catch a cold; where Tom off; Father's Block; or Jinny's Bread. Rich seaman's metaphors seem archaic today, but ones from cricket still crop up: when a ship goes by without stopping, which is a misfortune, they say 'Los' ball!' Their phraseology is quaint to us today: 'I gled fo meet you' (I am glad to meet you) or 'Tomolla ha tudder one' (the day after tomorrow).

lured to the outer world by better communications with it, had emigrated to New Zealand and the number who stayed loyal to Pitcairn had shrunk to 76. Not that the community is dying – far from it. So rich a heritage is not lightly put aside.

The looks of the Pitcairn islanders bear the mark of their heritage. Curiously, most observers, including the anthropologist Harry Shapiro (to whom anyone who writes about Pitcairn must be indebted), have remarked that the men look more English, while the women tend to look more Polynesian. Most of the people – men and women – have large prominent noses slightly beaked, heavy brows defined by bony bars above the eyes, giving the forehead a pronounced slope in profile. They are ruddy-complexioned and weather-beaten – again the

But the English did not have it all their own way. Many useful verbs are Tahitian. And the Tahitian love of repetition often doubles English words: illy-illy (hilly) means rough seas; boney-boney means skinny. They like to use rich Polynesian metaphors too: when a tired crew comes in, faces shiny with sweat, they say 'Here comes a boat of lanterns.' And there are Tahitian names for various plants and fish. Finally – and this too is a trait found in every aspect of Pitcairn life – they have invented words which owe nothing to either England or Polynesia, for example words for fish like 'pick-pick', 'whistlin' or 'dotter'.

The Anglo-Polynesian mixture is reflected in every aspect of life. In the early days, partly due to the preponderance of Tahitian women, partly because conditions were nearer to those of Tahiti than to those of England, there was probably more Polynesian culture on early Pitcairn. Houses had naval planked walls and were at first grouped round an English country-style 'green', but the roofs were Polynesian (now they are corrugated iron). Inside there was the Polynesian underground oven, there were calabashes and mats of tapa. In the evenings you saw by the faltering light of the *doodoee* candle-nut that crackled and spat as it burned. But the English sailors insisted on some furniture,

though most Polynesians like to sit on a matted floor. Beds were like ships' bunks, and there were heavy nautical chests and tables. Since nails were scarce, Pitcairners invented a shutter that slid open and shut along a groove – a good example of the islanders' inventiveness.

Like most Polynesians they grew and still grow yams, and many fruit-bearing trees which give a plentiful supply of bananas, coconuts, lemons, oranges – which are imported – grapefruits, mangoes, pineapples and passionfruit. The English contribution to agriculture was more in tools like the mattock and the hoe, and till recently the island's only form of wheeled transport – the wheelbarrow, specially designed for the rough hilly Pitcairn terrain.

Pitcairners eat Polynesian food with recipes handed down by the island's first housewives. They eat all the fruits mentioned above, as well as Irish and sweet potatoes (*kumara*), pumpkins, peas and sugar cane. One ever-popular blended dish is *pillihai* – boiled yams grated and mixed with coconut meat and sometimes sweetened with a syrup extracted from the *ti* plant that the unfortunate mutineer McCoy distilled. But in general – perhaps because of the early settlers' insular English distaste for unusual concoctions – Pitcairners like their

The exposed red volcanic soil shows erosion caused by the grazing of goats above Adamstown, Pitcairn's sole village and capital.

Pitcairners are strongly loyal to the British Crown and British traditions. They play cricket on a pitch made of coconut matting.

food in its simplest and purest elements. Nor do they like raw fish, which is thought a delicacy all over Polynesia.

At first both men and women wore Polynesian dress – the men, the *maro* loincloth; the women, skirts that were wrappings of tapa hung from the hips. But now dress is entirely European. In the 1930s women sometimes wore a frangipani flower behind the ear, but you would not witness that custom today.

Fishing is more a hobby than a chief source of food. They fish with tackle (made from the bark of a tree) and bait, like any Englishman on the edge of the Thames, but they enjoy spearing fish in the Polynesian way, and have the Tahitian knowledge of the moon's effect on tides and the consequent movement of fish. They never built Tahitian outriggers, but prefer English-style long-boats supposedly built after the one Queen Victoria presented them. Not surprisingly, they are fine boatmen. A small jetty has been built at Bounty Bay, and dangerous rocks have been dynamited, but boating prowess is still a requisite.

They once had pigs, but their religion has helped to

109

Len Brown holds a breadfruit – a source of nourishment – which he brought down from an inaccessible treetop by shooting away the stalk.

When cloth ran out on their
remote island, Pitcairn women
were content with grass skirts.
Contact has brought
bikinis and a motor-boat.

Tom Christian picks up news
from the outside world on
his ham radio – and cheers
up passing ships with news
from Pitcairn.

end pig-keeping. Early settlers' gardens were always threatened by wild hogs. Today a long controversy about the merits of goats is closing – with the anti-goat lobby winning the day. There are fewer and fewer goats, and the soil they have eroded stands a chance of recovery. Some say that goats provide meat for emergencies – in case of sudden isolation, but in general islanders rarely eat goat meat, and spurn the milk. Chicken are the most popular domestic animals.

Pitcairners' hobbies come from both England and Polynesia. They fly kites, play on swings, enjoy a traditional men versus the women tug-of-war once a year, which the women are allowed to win. Children spin tops, walk on stilts. Cricket follows makeshift rules. The pitch is on a slope, retrieving the ball is made tricky by wasps that lurk in the surrounding grass, but most important is that every family has representatives in both sides, so that every family will be among the defeated who are expected to provide the feast at the end of the day.

Pitcairn never had suffragettes. At first the women served food to their men, and thought it wrong to eat together. Yet the community was the first to have equal voting rights for all women and men over 18 years old.

The system of land distribution is a good example of English culture, with its emphasis on 'mine and thine' and general possessiveness, combining with Tahitians' stronger sense of community and sharing. Following Christian's system, families started with equal amounts of land, which was inherited by all the children of the family both male and female. As some families were large and some small, some Pitcairners had a large slice of land, while others had hardly any. So – more along Tahitian lines – the land-starved could 'borrow' land rent-free from a neighbor. Nevertheless, the compromise is not completely satisfactory, and the landless are often among those who emigrate. With more Europeanization there is less 'borrowing'.

The trade system also exemplifies the Anglo-Polynesian blend. There is a hurried collection of fruit by all the islanders when a ship appears, and the goods exchanged for the fruit are shared out. But the conditions for sale of other goods like curios is 'each man for himself'. The boats go out to the steamer as quickly as possible and the islanders press their wares on everyone aboard the big ship. But again, community sense comes in: the islanders have a strict rotation system whereby each man spends a certain length of time looking after the rowboats below while his fellows ply their trade above. Hand in hand with private enterprise goes compulsory public work for all men between 16 and 60. Pitcairners own all the boats communally, and haul them ashore together, now assisted by a motor.

Community life is directed by a huge bell that hangs from a cross bar in the village square. When a series of double clangs ring out, it is time for church. Three clangs mean a public meeting; four – a share-out; and five – a ship is arriving. The bell, together with the *Bounty* anchor, is in the one village square bounded by the church, the magistrate's office and courthouse, and a bench where veterans and youths alike loiter for gossip and fun.

Religion is a binding force, and has been since the days of Adams. But the conversion of the whole island by Seventh Day Adventists in 1887 has kept alight the islanders' zeal. Whether they have ever suffered the taint of sanctimony is debated, but most observers say Pitcairners are sincere and free from hypocrisy. They drink no alcohol, eat no pork. Long graces are said before meals. They pay tithes to the church, with contributions of fruit rotting untouched in a hut. Collections for charity (ironical, since the islanders themselves often receive goods from the USA and elsewhere) are very large. Religious zest made the islanders famous in Victorian days, largely because their apparent chastity, which they equated with morality, was in sharp contrast to the promiscuity of their distant cousins in Tahiti and many parts of Polynesia. But the 'purity' of the islanders and the 'free living' of other Polynesians have both been exaggerated.

The islanders elect a magistrate, to be assisted by two councillors, every third Christmas. He settles disputes, checks landmarks, and is the acknowledged leader of the community. But there is little need for iron-fisted law on Pitcairn, and the tiny prison has hardly ever been occupied. There are problems on Pitcairn as everywhere, and it is foolish to make it sound idyllic. The subsistence economy has been backed up by British aid, and above all by the sale of Pitcairn postage stamps. Otherwise the islanders would be very poor. Their richest resource is not the lush but limited soil and the fair climate, but their history of romance and adventure. A Victorian traveler's report that 'direful social convulsions and carking cares are unknown' is false. Yet a living descendant of the *Bounty* mutineers is right when he says: 'Fletcher Christian he find a good place to hide.'

Juan Fernandez
Robinson Crusoe's island

For four years of the 18th
century, the sole inhabitant
was Alexander Selkirk, who
inspired Defoe. Now a mixed
race of lobstermen live here.

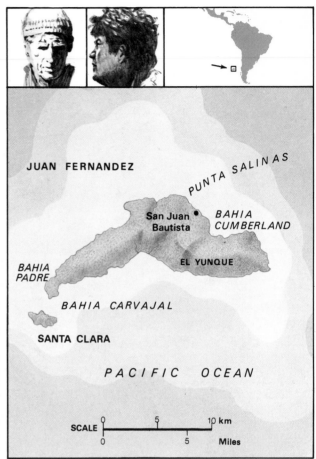

In a work devoted to the peoples of the world – so many of them, in so many different places, leading such very diverse lives – it might be appropriate to pause for a moment, and remember the uniqueness and the solitude of each individual.

And it is here, in the volume that concerns itself with the world and peoples of the Pacific Ocean, that an interlude of this kind most properly belongs. The Pacific Ocean, the ocean of peace; and when we hear the words, there springs into the mind at once an image vaguely built up from our childhood reading, an image of the vast blue sea and of some small island, of solitude and serenity. The vision tugs at our fevered hearts: in imagination, we lie there in that little palm-leaf hut, well fed with roast pork and with vaguely-imagined tropical fruits, and night falls suddenly, while the breakers thunder on the distant coral reef. The peoples of the world seem blessedly very far away.

It is a dream that corresponds to something very deep in ourselves. 'Humanity' is, after all, an abstraction. Only people are real; and each one looks out from the prison of his own self, through the windows of his eyes, and gazes with mixed feelings upon the proliferation and pressure of his fellow humans. We are certainly social

113

(Top) Except for a few castaways Más á Tierra, discovered by Juan Fernandez in 1563, was uninhabited for most of the 19th century.

(Bottom) For these Spanish speaking children future employment prospects, besides fishing, include a job with the naval radio station.

animals, and we have a strong tendency to crowd together in cities, even to our own great disadvantage: 'No man is an Island, entire of itself' wrote Donne. But that was never the whole truth, and Arnold saw the other side of the matter:

> Yes: in the sea of life enisled,
> With echoing straits between us thrown,
> Dotting the shoreless watery wild,
> We mortal millions live alone.

It seems likely that in certain more primitive societies the sense of social identity is felt more strongly, the sense of individual self more feebly. But in modern western society there prevails this dream or nostalgia of solitude, of total privacy, of an earth without other peoples, populated simply by oneself. It is a dream that fascinates, since it renders incarnate an ultimate fact about ourselves; and so it becomes a literary archetype, haunting the mind. We dream of desert islands, and the poets and story-tellers do their best to feed this powerful appetite of the imagination.

It is an appetite that has always existed, but perhaps more intensely during these last two hundred years, a time during which the pressures of civilization have become steadily more grievous. It grows by what it feeds on; and there have always been stories of island solitude to tug at the dissatisfied mind. But at the beginning of the 18th century, the dream or archetype suddenly became concrete in a new and vivid way, deeply interesting as mere fact, and for that reason deeply stimulating to the imagination. And now whatever other hopes and fantasies we may entertain, there is a secret part of us which identifies for ever with Alexander Selkirk and with Robinson Crusoe.

The happy island of solitude, so potent in dream, actually exists in the most mundane and geographical sense. Leave the coast of Chile and journey out into the Ocean of Peace, and about five hundred miles off Valparaiso you will find the islands of Juan Fernandez, named after the Spanish navigator who discovered them in 1563. There are three of them: Más á Tierra (Spanish for nearer land) which is about 36 square miles in area; tiny Santa Clara alongside, and Más Afuera (further out), which is about 33 square miles and does indeed lie about a hundred miles further out to the west.

These are volcanic islands, mountainous out of all proportion to their size: on Más á Tierra a wedge-shaped crag called El Yunque ('the Anvil') rises to three thousand feet, while the summit of Más Afuera – Los Innocentes – is more than twice as high. The landscape is 'romantick' in the best taste of the 18th century, with springs and waterfalls and ravines; in Selkirk's time the islands were thickly wooded all over, but the valuable sandalwood and the *chonta* palm have been cropped so heavily that their lower levels are now bare and exposed.

They have been occupied intermittently and on a small scale since their first discovery. In 1750 they were

(Top) A plaque commemorates Alexander Selkirk, voluntary castaway here from 1704-1708. After hearing Selkirk's story Defoe wrote *Robinson Crusoe*.

(Bottom) Cumberland Bay is the only safe anchorage on the island: here most of the islanders live in the village of San Juan Bautista.

garrisoned for a time by Spain in response to a threat of British occupation. When Chile became independent in 1810 they came under the jurisdiction of that country, and they retain that status, being regarded for administrative purposes as part of Valparaiso. They were sometimes used as a penal settlement, but were totally uninhabited for long periods during the 19th century. They are now inhabited by a few people of Chilean origin – 501 of them in 1960 – who are concentrated in the village of San Juan Bautista on Más á Tierra, where they live mostly by fishing for lobster and exporting them to the mainland. Apart from their wooden houses, the village includes an elementary school, the ruins of an 18th century Spanish fort, the sheds of the companies which export the lobsters, a lighthouse, a chapel, and a cemetery. There is also a monument to those who died in the *Dresden*, a German ship which survived the Battle of the Falkland Islands in 1914, but sank off Más á Tierra. A naval radio station and a minor tourist industry provide the people with a little further employment.

Memorably, though not uniquely, these islands have a history of solitary occupation. In 1680 the buccaneer Captain William Dampier, pursued by the Spanish, was obliged to leave the islands hurriedly and to leave behind him a Moskito Indian; four years later he returned and picked up the castaway, who had managed his affairs meanwhile in a very practical way, sawing up a gun to make harpoons, knives and fish-hooks, building a wooden hut and lining it with goatskins. When his rescuers arrived he killed three goats so as to be able to greet them with a banquet. These animals, so important for the later image of the islands, had been introduced by Juan Fernandez himself when he first came, so that passing ships would be able to provision themselves with fresh meat. Later on there was another castaway, this time a survivor of shipwreck: he spent five years alone on Más á Tierra before being rescued by a passing ship.

But the most famous of all castaways was Alexander Selkirk, a Scottish sailor and – it appears – a thoroughly quarrelsome man. He was born at Largo in Fife. and ran away to sea at the age of 19 after getting into trouble with the kirk. Six years later he came home, quarrelled with his brothers, and at once went back to sea. In 1703 he sailed as sailing master of the *Cinque Ports*, an English privateering galley under Dampier's command, but by the time of their arrival off Juan Fernandez next year he had quarreled so violently with his commander that he was marooned – at his own suggestion – on Más á Tierra. This was in September 1704.

Four years and four months later, two other English privateers were sailing in those waters, under the command of Captain Woodes Rogers. He decided to land on the Juan Fernandez islands for water, and also, as it turned out, to collect a harvest of shellfish. The night before they landed, he and his crew saw lights on Más á Tierra, and took them to be the lights of a French ship;

Juan Fernandez Robinson Crusoe's island

The ancestors of these permanent settlers arrived from Chile in the 19th century to an island uninhabited from time immemorial.

Goats were originally imported by Juan Fernandez to feed castaways. People value them highly. This dog a killer, has been hanged.

in fact they were Selkirk's watch fires. He was found next day and brought on board in his goatskins, 'looking wilder than the first owners of them', and so unaccustomed to human company and to speech that his broken Scots English was almost unintelligible to his listeners.

Selkirk soon adapted himself however, and sailed away as mate of Roger's ship the *Duke*, arriving hime in 1711. He seems to have acquired a taste for solitude, and regretted his return to the haunts of men. In spite of the lavish £800 which was his share in the *Duke's* prize-money, he declared that he had been happier when penniless on the island. He returned to his parents' village and home, built himself a cave as a hermitage in their garden, and there and on solitary walks sought repose in solitude. Eventually, after further trouble with the elders of the kirk, he went back to sea and died in 1723.

His fame was achieved in three stages. In 1712 Rogers published his book *A Cruising Voyage Round the World,* which gave an account of Selkirk's rescue and brought his name to public attention; in particular, he was interviewed by Richard Steele the essayist, and the outcome was a paper in *The Englishman* (1713) from which most of our knowledge of him is derived. We learn of his early repentance, his melancholy and despair on the island, and then of his gradual recovery of spirits. He set to work, built two huts, kept count of the days, sang psalms and prayed, became by his own reckoning a better Christian than before or afterwards; he fed richly upon turtles, craw-fish, goat's meat, turnips, and wild plums; he made goatskin garments, and hammered hoop-iron into a knife. On one occasion he fell a hundred feet and lay unconscious for a time which – by observing the moon – he afterwards reckoned as three days and nights. Rats were his worst enemy, and cats were his defense.

After the publication of this paper, Selkirk was interviewed by many curious people; and it is likely, though not certain, that Daniel Defoe was one of them. However that may be, it was directly because of Selkirk's story, as reported by Steele, that there appeared in 1719 *The Life and Strange Surprizing Adventures of Robinson Crusoe, of York, Mariner.*

We need not be concerned here with the literary appraisal of this famous work, and its importance for the history of the novel. But its immediate success and its permanent popularity show that it touched a nerve and met an imaginative need. It has been translated into at least thirty languages, including Yiddish, Gaelic, Turkish, Persian, and Polynesian, and during the 19th century two abridged versions or paraphrases were written in Latin, in order to allure the reluctant schoolboy. Furthermore, it has been very widely imitated – slavishly by some second-rate 18th century authors, more loosely by the more creative later on – so that in varying degrees it has been the inspiration and model for any number of major and minor classics. Its influence can be detected obviously enough in *The Swiss Family*

Robinson, but also in Ballantyne's *Coral Island*, in *Masterman Ready*, in *Mr Midshipman Easy*, in *Treasure Island*, in *Enoch Arden*, in *The Gold Bug*, and in countless minor works right up to our own time.

The dream haunts us still. In some developed and specialized version strict solitude is not appropriate. If it is to be used for some allegory of the human condition, the island will need a small population – the strangely mixed-up characters on Prospero's island, for example, or the schoolboys of *The Lord of the Flies* or the developing society of Rose Macaulay's *Orphan Island*. Even Crusoes are not always solitary. Some Man Friday may turn up, however improbably in Crusoe's own case.

But even in the story it is the solitude that charms, even if it is a shared solitude. When native war-canoes and pirate ships intrude upon the coral island, the dream is dissipated. For its full functioning it depends upon an unintentional and undesired marooning. The man who takes refuge on his island by full and free choice, as Selkirk did at a moment of folly, may be a mere misanthrope, a hater of mankind like the minority of sullen recluses who have always existed everywhere. Alternatively he may be a hermit, fleeing from men in order to be alone with God. And there is a long story here, from St John the Divine seeing his fiery visions on the island of Patmos, through the countless hermits whose ruined huts still carry a fragrance of old holiness on countless small islands around the coasts of Britain, and up to Monsignor Hawes, the priest who in our own time became known as 'the hermit of Cat Island' in the Bahamas.

But the mere misanthrope is a dull unattractive fellow, and the purely religious hermit seeks a life beyond the reach of most of us. The dream, the visionary adventure lies in the idea of finding oneself unexpectedly and unintentionally on some small island – well-stocked, agreeable in climate, off the shipping and airline routes, preferably in the Pacific.

How would you respond if it actually happened? The possibility is not altogether remote. Airplanes sometimes crash in remote waters, each one has a life-jacket, you might be the one survivor, and warm currents might drift you towards that golden virgin beach, those clear springs, those fruit-trees, those goats.

In the event, would you go to pieces? Would you go quietly mad, all alone there in your easy-living paradise?

If it happens, take Burton's advice and avoid idleness. Make rules for yourself. Invent tasks. Man is an uphill animal.

117

Maori and white New Zealanders

While industries grow in the
cities, this mountain deer
hunter lives the kind of
rugged life familiar to the
early settlers of the 1840s.

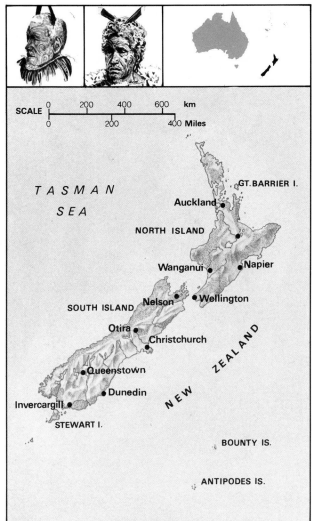

TASMAN SEA

GT. BARRIER I.

Auckland

NORTH ISLAND

Wanganui   Napier

Nelson   Wellington

SOUTH ISLAND

Otira

Christchurch

NEW ZEALAND

Queenstown

Dunedin

Invercargill

STEWART I.

BOUNTY IS.

ANTIPODES IS.

A signpost on the northernmost cape of New Zealand wryly reads 'Buff (southernmost tip of New Zealand) 745 miles, Equator 2,065 miles, Sydney 1,065 miles, Suva 1,030 miles, Panama 6,579 miles'. New Zealand is a new country. The indigenous inhabitants, the Maori, probably started to arrive about 1000 AD, but nobody knows the exact date. And settlers from England did not arrive in any great numbers until after 1840. In spite of a relatively short history as a nation New Zealanders have achieved much, materially and culturally. Today's white New Zealander is no longer an Englishman abroad: he has a new and recognizable identity and a strong sense of independence.

The two long narrow islands of New Zealand, North Island and South Island, are just over 100,000 square miles, and inhabited by only about three million people, and stand end to end, anchored as a New Zealand poet wrote 'like a child's kite in the indifferent blue'. New Zealand is one of the southernmost land areas of the world and an isolated country. Australia, its nearest 119

Maoris and white New Zealanders

Pilot and hunter load the slaughtered deer aboard the plane after a precarious landing in lonely Westland valley on South Island.

Towards the end of November the farmer and his men ride up into the hills with their dogs and bring the sheep down into the valley for shearing.

neighbor, is a thousand miles away to the north-west.

Running through New Zealand's growth and development as a country are three firmly interwoven threads. The strongest of these is the land itself; its yield and ownership has always been the main preoccupation of both Maori and European settlers. The second thread is that two peoples, each with its own distinctive culture, arrived to settle and become New Zealanders. And the third thread, which has emerged particularly strongly in this century, is the dependence of New Zealanders on their Welfare State. This dependence started as far back in the story of New Zealand as the struggle for land and the overwhelming necessity for the Maori and white settler to live together peaceably.

The land itself was the beginning. New Zealand in legend and history has been 'discovered' several times. It has been established from carbon dating that some Polynesians lived along the New Zealand coast by 1000 AD. But the Maoris have their own legend which tells that their ancestors arrived in big outrigger canoes about twenty-four generations ago – probably about 1350. The legend tells that they came to New Zealand from Hawaiki (perhaps Tahiti) as a result of an earlier visit by Kupe, a Hawaiki fisherman. One day when Kupe was out fishing a giant octopus attacked his bait. Kupe chased the octopus and when at long last he caught up with it and killed it he found himself in the narrow strait that divides North and South Island. He landed on South Island, and after a short stay sailed up the west coast of North Island, finally sailing for his distant home from an inlet on North Auckland. He named this inlet *Hokianga nui a Kupe*, 'Great Returning Place of Kupe'. When he reached home he told people of the marvels that awaited them on the two islands he had visited. After a while the Maoris, with a great fleet of canoes each carrying 250 people, set sail to emigrate to the new country. They followed Kupe's navigational instructions and, so their legend says, after a heroic and hazard-ridden voyage reached the shores of New Zealand. Most of their canoes landed on North Island, and they have lived mainly there ever since. Today two thirds of the

The wool of these sheep awaiting shearing will become part of the farm produce which makes up 90 per cent of New Zealand's exports.

(Right) Young Maori enjoy the warmth of a thermal pool at Whakarewarewa but others come for their healing virtues to the nearby sanatorium.

Maoris and white New Zealanders

The British-style uniform of caps and blazers worn by students at Christ's College in Christchurch is evidence of the origins of the settlers.

Maori live in the north of North Island. This great voyage of more than 2,000 miles across stormy seas without charts or navigational instruments has been remembered and celebrated by Maori poets and song-writers throughout the centuries. And the names of the voyaging canoes, *Tainui, Arawa, Aotea* and *Tokomaru*, remain as tribe names today.

There are other theories as to how the Maori reached New Zealand: the Polynesians were skilled sailors but only rarely undertook transoceanic voyages and it seems more likely that the Maori canoes were blown off-course on a fishing expedition or on an inter-island voyage.

Whether or not their voyage to New Zealand was intentional the Maori did not attempt to sail back. They settled in the land they named *Aotearoa*, 'Land of the Long White Cloud' and lived there in complete isolation for about three hundred years. The first European to 'discover' New Zealand was a Dutchman, Abel Tasman, in 1642. He sailed along part of the coast and attempted a landing; but after a skirmish with the Maori in which some of his men were killed he withdrew. On his return to Holland he gave an unfavorable report of the island. He did however give the country its name – Nieuw Zeeland – after a province in Holland. Another 127 years passed before New Zealand was 'discovered' again. This time it was Captain Cook in 1769 who, after visiting Tahiti, sailed south and landed at many places around

122

Glaciered mountains rib South Island. Light planes serve well as transport. There are 8,000 airstrips for one of the least populated lands.

the New Zealand coast. There is a famous old story which says that when Cook's sailors rowed ashore in their longboats the Maori thought they were spirits or goblins because, unlike the Maori, who faced the way they rowed, these men sat with their backs the way they were going and therefore must have had eyes in the backs of their heads!

After Cook met and traded with the Maori he wrote in his journal 'The Natives of this country are Strong, rawboned, well made active people, rather under the common size, especially the Men; they are of a very dark colour, with black hair, thin black beards, and white teeth and such as do not disfigure their faces with tattowing, etc have in general very good features. The Men generally wear their Hair long, Coomb'd up, and tied upon the Crown of their Heads; some of the women were it long and loose upon their shoulders, old women especially; others again wear it crop't short . . . They seem to enjoy a good state of Health, and many of them live to a good old Age.'

Cook estimated that there were about 200,000 Maori, divided into about fifty tribes. Today the Maori number 230,000, nearly 10 per cent of New Zealand's population. Each tribe, with its own set of common ancestors who according to Maori legend would all have arrived in the same canoe, was subdivided into *hapuu*, clans with a common ancestor. And within the *hapuu* the Maori lived in extended family groups.

The Maori used the whole island for their sustenance. Where the soil was fertile they cultivated *kumara*, the sweet potato, which they had brought with them. They collected edible tree-roots and berries, fished for eels and crayfish and collected fresh-water mussels. They also ate each other. The Maori were notorious cannibals, who kept their victims in pens to fatten them up. They used the dense bush that covered North Island to build their huts, and palisades to protect their tribal villages, and to construct canoes. The Maori divided work fairly equally between men and women: the men did the harder, more exacting work – tree-climbing, fishing, fowling, and breaking up the ground for new crops, while the women weeded the soil, collected shellfish, plaited mats, wove clothes and cooked two daily meals.

The Maori believed not in one supreme god, but in many gods and spirits, called *atua*. Trees, birds, fish, houses and many other things were believed to have their own spirits which had to be protected from sorcery. Although they acknowledged the spirit who created them as the most powerful of the *atua*, they felt closest to the spirits of their ancestors, who gave force to black magic and enforced customs and law by *tapu* (taboo). The Maori saw the universe as being made up of two

Like most houses those rising above the Wellington marina are built of wood. As a precaution against earthquakes few are over two storeys high.

Maoris and white New Zealanders

New Zealand's rugged forests attract hunters and fishermen. Others prefer racing keeler boats off Auckland, New Zealand's biggest city.

124

Aluminium, steel, oil and gas industries are reducing New Zealand's dependence on imports. Parts of Wellington are as industrialized as any large city.

Any New Zealander, even this
construction worker on a
Wellington motorway, can see
the Prime Minister personally
if he wishes.

Their country has been settled
for only a hundred years, but
these youngsters are growing
up in a country with a strong
sense of national identity.

opposing yet complementary spheres called *tapu* and *noa*. Harmony in the universe and of man in his relation to it was brought about by a correct relationship between the spheres of *tapu* and *noa*. All activities were regulated by the ritual demands of these two forces and the success of any undertaking depended to a large extent on the proper relationship of the person and his material with these powers in the universe.

It was into this isolated and well-established society that the first British settlers came in ever-increasing numbers, bringing their own religions and culture. Sealers and whalers were among the first people to exploit the newly discovered land. Methodist, Anglican and Roman Catholic missionaries followed quickly, and in 1840 the New Zealand Company founded by an Englishman, Edward Gibbon Wakefield, set up its first colony of British settlers on the site that is now Wellington, the capital of New Zealand. In the same year Captain Hobson, acting for the British colonial office, persuaded many of the powerful Maori chiefs to sign the Treaty of Waitanga. This treaty made New Zealand a British colony and promised protection of Maori lands, forests, and fishing rights.

The land that attracted the settlers to New Zealand is a rugged mountainous country with peaks soaring above 7,000 feet. There are earthquakes, live volcanoes and geysers, where the earth itself seems to boil. There are immense stretches of forests, lakes, swift-flowing rivers, and sandy beaches sometimes fifty miles long. The climate is temperate: much of the country has about 2,000 hours of sunshine a year and the sun shines often in winter. It is an ideal climate for people, and indeed creatures of any sort, to live in. But most of all there is grass – English grass and natural tussock which covers the hillside. For New Zealanders today this grass turns their sheep into wool, lamb, mutton, and their cows into milk, butter and cheese, most of it for export.

A New Zealand farmer either has a sheep farm or a dairy farm – there are few mixed farms. Most are worked by their owners – often with help from the family, supported by a little hired help. Roughly a quarter of all farms are leased from the state; the rest are freehold. New Zealand sheep farms are much alike. The farmer's homestead, built of wood with an iron roof painted red, is usually built on flat ground surrounded by hedges and trees. A small distance away are the orchard, a few beehives, the chicken yard and the dog kennels. Nearby on most farms is the woolshed where the sheep are sheared. Unless it is the season for dipping or shearing the farmer leaves his sheep to graze and get fat on the spurs and ridges of the surrounding hills.

The sheep farmer's year moves in well-defined seasons. August and September is the lambing season when the farmer and his men keep a watchful eye on the thousands of newly born lambs. The weak ones can then be brought back to the farmhouse to be reared by hand from a 125 bottle. As the sun grows stronger and the snow on the mountains begins to melt, the sheep and their lambs scatter higher and higher in search of grazing. At the end of November and throughout December the farmer and his men go off on horseback, followed by their dogs, up into the hills to herd the sheep down to the farm for shearing. When they have reached the highest peak they divide up and each man takes a ridge. At a given signal each man starts riding down his ridge and at once the sheep start to move, urged on by the highly trained sheepdogs. As the shepherds descend the hills the flocks become larger and larger until there are strings of sheep running quickly, all heading down the valley to the farm. Safely yarded, the sheep are ready to be shorn.

If the sheep are dry the men begin to shear immediately. The machines whir in the skilful hands of the shearers – they peel back the soft fleeces from the sheep's skins, working at tremendous speed. When the fleece is off, the 'picker-up' gathers the wool up and throws it on to a table where he skirts it with rapid machine-like movements. He folds it into a soft ball and passes it to a man who controls the press. When the wool is baled and marked with the station brand, it is transported to the wool stores in the cities where it is classed according to its quality, rebaled and prepared for sale or export.

Although shearing time is perhaps the busiest time for the New Zealand sheep farmer, he is fully occupied for the rest of the year. His sheep must be dipped, fat lambs (three to eight months old) taken from the fields to be slaughtered for export, and his land top-dressed with fertilizers. New Zealand leads the world in the use of airplanes to drop top dressing on pasture land. Planes operating off eight thousand airstrips drop fertilizer on five million acres of land every year. The soil has been completely rebuilt from the condition in which the first English settlers found it, and today New Zealanders use two-thirds of their mountainous country for farming.

New Zealand has a predominantly farming economy: farm products account for nearly 90 per cent of exports. But the people are always open to new ways of exploiting the resources their land offers. In recent years they have begun producing aluminium and steel for export, and deposits of oil and gas have been found off the coast of North Island in big enough quantities to give New Zealanders hope for self-sufficiency. They also manufacture goods of a variety out of all proportion to their small population: hydraulic trench diggers, acrylic paint, bicycles, ships, gin, adhesives and many other things. They manufacture farm machinery, newsprint, woodwork equipment, lawn-mowers and carpets, all for export. For a small and relatively new nation New Zealand is very independent.

New Zealand has the charm of being small, intimate and expanding without ever giving a feeling of being crowded. Even in the four main cities – Dunedin, Christchurch, Auckland and Wellington, the capital,

Even today a Maori chief
must be skilled in oratory,
expert in genealogies and
ceremonial procedure, like
his forefathers of the 1880s.

most city buildings are only two storeys high. Although New Zealand's periodic earthquakes are one reason for low-built architecture, there is always unlimited room for a city to expand outwards. Most houses are built of wood and nearly every house has its own garden back and front. New Zealanders do not tolerate high density living – every man has his own quarter acre. One out of three people owns a car; car-owners tend to keep their cars for ten or twenty years as they are very expensive. If possible a New Zealand family, out of love for the outdoor life, will also buy a beach or mountain weekend house. Many people spend their weekends and holidays fishing, walking, ski-ing, hunting and yachting, although easily the most popular sports in New Zealand are rugby football and horse-racing.

There is no doubt that New Zealanders universally enjoy a life of ease and prosperity. Their highly developed welfare state looks after everybody. Pensions for the old and disabled are generous. A free medical service has been in operation since the 1930s. There are cheap government-subsidized mortgages and a family benefit program that gives mothers $1.50 a week for each child, and also allows a family to borrow against child benefits to finance the buying of a house. Farmers get loans, cheap fertilizer and pesticides and transport subsidies. Education is free and there are government-ordered wage boosts to keep pace with inflation. This form of society leads to one of New Zealand's strongest characteristics – egalitarianism. Servants are virtually unknown; artisans, laborers, businessmen all live together in the same districts. A man calls his boss by his first name. Democracy is carried to the ultimate. Any New Zealander can see his own member of parliament and prime minister without the slightest difficulty.

It is an integrated way of life which, considering its youth, has become stable and established remarkably quickly and to which the indigenous Maori, the older New Zealanders, have by and large successfully adapted, although the beginnings of the new relationship were possibly ominous for the Maori. When the settlers came in the 19th century changes followed so fast that by the end of the century much of Maori culture and way of life had virtually disappeared. They lost most of their land to the white settlers. They had to adapt to the pressures and demands of a new economy.

But their culture has survived in part and today Maori people, although New Zealanders working as farmers, school teachers, mechanics, sheep shearers (they are the best), members of parliament and many other professions, keep their own culture and traditions. There is so much integration between white New Zealanders and Maoris that many white New Zealanders claim to have more Maori blood than they really have in order to be identified as Maori rather than as white.

The Maori no longer live in the extended family groups of pre-Pakeha (European) days. Today they live in single

(Top) Maori no longer tattoo their faces and bodies but the ancient designs are still painted on for special festivals and ceremonies.

(Bottom) The traditional circular designs used by the tattooist have important *tapu* (religious) meanings and can only be executed by a man.

Maori were cannibal warriors who increased their enemies' fear of them with ferocious expressions, and kept victims in pens to fatten up.

By the 1880s the Maori population was fast dwindling. Once 200,000, by 1896 it was 46,000. But now it has climbed back to 230,000.

The carved greenstone figures around this girl's neck are characteristic of the stylized forms in traditional Maori art.

Maori women traditionally plaited geometric designs in their mats while the men's carvings and tattooing patterns were curvilinear.

family groups, although families still have close relationships with other families with whom they claim descent from a common ancestor, some two to four generations removed. This large family group often owns land communally, has its own family club, possibly its own *marae* or community courtyard, and has an acknowledged head – usually the oldest male in the senior generation. Members of the group help each other in many daily activities as well as in time of need, and with public celebrations such as weddings and funerals.

Because Maori households tend to be scattered, the facilities of the *marae* give a focus for their community life and the opportunity to display the lavish hospitality for which Maori communities are famous.

Families from communities all around are invited to celebrations. The *marae* consists of several buildings – a meeting house, a dining hall and a courtyard in front of the meeting house, which is the *marae* proper. Here the Maori hold debates on community and inter-community affairs. And it is here that visitors are welcomed and the dead farewelled. The meeting house is often beautifully 129

Maoris and white New Zealanders

This *marae* or family meeting
house was built in the late
19th century when Maori wood
carving reached its peak.
The art has now declined.

130

decorated inside and out with traditional carvings and has a special meaning for the Maori. Inside, where guests are entertained to weddings and twenty-first birthday parties, are carved stylized figures of ancestors. When a Maori enters a meeting house he feels that he is entering the bosom of his ancestors.

Maori call *marae* gatherings *hui*. The *hui tangi*, the funeral wake, is the ceremony that the Maori hold in the greatest respect. It lasts for three or four days during which the relatives all come to pay their respects to the dead person, who lies in state in the *marae*. Throughout the wake the elders make speeches and chant poetry. After the body has been buried there is a great feast to relieve the intense mourning. Although the Maori belong to Anglican, Roman Catholic, Methodist, Mormon or Presbyterian churches, they associate death with their old belief of *tapu* (taboo). A Maori is buried with his personal possessions and among many Maori it is customary for them to sprinkle themselves with water after attending the burial. An important ceremony after the burial is held at the home of the deceased to free it from *tapu* and make it habitable again. The final mortuary ceremony takes place months later when a headstone is ceremonially unveiled.

Since World War II New Zealand has become more and more industrialized and more and more people are drawn into cities to work, and it is urbanization rather than Pakeha that has most transformed the traditional life of the Maori. Rural poverty, shortage of land and a high birthrate have forced them to leave the *marae* for jobs in the cities. Urbanization has for the first time brought Maori and Pakeha into close social contact. New Zealand is committed to an ideology of racial equality, and government policy since 1960 has been to integrate Maori rural immigrants into urban life. The problem for the Maori is to integrate while if possible resisting pressures to assimilate.

While they attempt to adapt their culture to urban life, urban Maori try to keep a strong sense of their identity. First generation migrants especially often go home for holidays and *hui*, maintaining links with their rural communities. And rural relatives are never short of accommodation when they visit the city. Maori family clubs and tribal associations are set up in the cities to emphasize the importance of kinship links in their new environment. Culture clubs for Maori youth are very common in the cities and every year the members of these clubs compete in cultural festivals held all over the country. They build urban *marae*. These serve the social function of mediating between different social groups and also between urban and rural *marae*. The tribal associations, culture clubs and urban *marae* are the institutions through which the urban Maori can adapt their traditional culture. By transposing their culture the Maori are able to make their own distinctive contribution to urban life.

133

(Top) A terracotta totem outside their bungalow symbolizes the strong feeling this modern Maori family still have for their tribal identity.

Women of the Tuhoe tribe, Ruatoki, gather on the steps of their *marae*. Like many older Maori, they wear *moko*, chin tattoos.

Nauruans
Micronesia

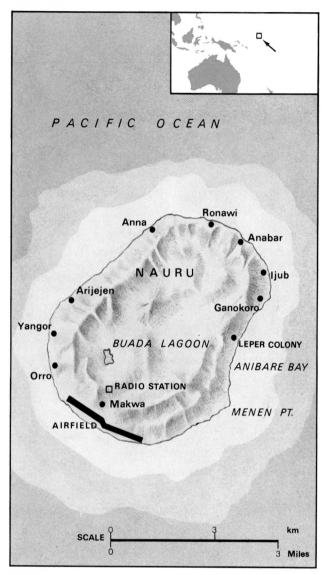

shrubs, certainly no homes. For the island plateau is made mostly of phosphate, which provides the islanders with almost all their wealth and activity. All day mechanical grabs scratch and claw the lime soil for the rich phosphate that makes the best fertilizer in the world. As the phosphate is extracted from the rock, only the occasional pinnacle of coral – sometimes fifty feet high – is left untouched by the bulldozers. All around is rubble.

Nauruans benefit from this devastation. They have the highest per capita income in the world – on average, over $6,500 a year for every man, woman and child. But this is misleading. The costs of phosphate production are very high. But more important, a third of the island's phosphate has already been exhausted. By 1992, the whole lot will probably have disappeared, together with a large physical portion of the once-beautiful island.

All at once the Nauruans themselves realized that the phosphate that dominates the life on the island was not an unqualified blessing. In 1939 the Council of Chiefs had their first worries about the long-term future of their island, then administered by Australia under a League of Nations Trusteeship. (Nauru was formerly a German colony.) Ironically, it was perhaps this new fear that brought Nauruans together, faced with a common problem, and led to independence in 1968, making their new republic the smallest sovereign state in the world.

The indigenous Nauruans are nearest to the Polynesians in stock. They are thick-set, with large imposing faces and unknown origins. They belonged to clans, and traced their descent through females. In the 1840s they had a queen. They believed in a mighty goddess called Eijebong, and made her offerings. They talked in tones of awe about an island of the spirits called Buitani which resembled Nauru but was bigger.

Friction among the twelve clans was centuries old, but the balance of power was upset when the white man brought the gun, and when the Gilbert Islanders brought a coconut toddy called *ekarawe*. These events led to the Ten Years War which started in 1878. It was so bloody and destructive that the population was in danger of

Nauru, or Pleasant Island, is a tiny round speck that lies quite alone in the western Pacific Ocean. Its nearest neighbor is Ocean Island, 190 miles to the east. Another two hundred miles further on is the main chain of the Gilbert Islands. It is the smallest independent country in the world. It is also richest in terms of per capita income.

The republic of Nauru (pronounced Now-Roo) is encircled by reefs and shaped like a hat. The narrow coastal brim, twelve miles round, is fringed with coconut palms. The soft pink and creamy frangipani, the flaming poinsettia and the scarlet splash of the hibiscus make this brim a delight to eyes and nose.

But the crown of the hat presents a different scene – one that has been likened to the moon. The center of Nauru, a plateau two hundred feet above the sea, has been devastated by bulldozers – there are no trees, no

32

(Top) The world's smallest sovereign state is digging itself away. Loading phosphates at the cantilevers stops only when the sea is stormy.

extinction. The Europeans eventually brought peace and order. But they also brought a more powerful culture. Nauruans have largely adopted the white man's ways.

Nevertheless the Nauruans maintain their traditional fondness for keeping tame frigate birds. Some spend many hours plotting to capture this rare, precious bird, planting life-like decoys and catching them with deadly accurate lassos. Once secured they tie up the bird for six weeks until it is tame. Then it can be used as a decoy to help its proud owner build up a team of frigate birds. Great prestige can be gained by displaying a fine collection of these birds; sons gladly inherit them when their fathers die. It is unfortunate for the Nauruans that they eat too many of the limited supply of fish, so keeping frigate birds is no longer officially encouraged.

But there is nothing wrong with the Noddy Hunt, another old pastime that survives. With long poles that hold giant butterfly nets, parties of hunters set off at sundown to the woods that fringe the island. Nauruans can mimic the Noddies (or Black Tern) with uncanny precision. The Noddies – sometimes 150 in an evening – fly into the nets. To Nauruans they are delicious.

The Nauruans' present dependence on imported goods

and their European life-style all date from 1798 when Captain John Fearn visited the island. He was the first European to set foot on Nauru. In 1842 an English remittance man named Harris married a Nauruan girl and produced a large family. As early as 1843 another English captain recorded that 'This island is infested by Europeans who are either runaway convicts, or deserters from whalers . . . and for the most part men of the very worst description.' A few years later Nauruans massacred the crew of an American brig after a coconut dispute.

Calmer relations with the outer world started with the German annexation of 1888, though little was done to develop the island's resources. At the turn of the century missionaries revolutionized Nauruan life by banning polygamy and most traditional rites and dances.

By 1905 large-scale phosphate mining had begun. The demand for labor led to the import of Chinese and Gilbertese – and dysentery, infantile paralysis, yaws,

leprosy and the malarial mosquito. Of today's 6,000 Nauruans, nearly two-thirds are of indigenous stock, while the rest are from other islands or are Europeans. The thousand Chinese are ineligible for citizenship.

This racial mixing has inevitably undermined the old culture. The Ten Years War of the last century, the sudden switch from German to Australian government during World War I, the hardships of conquest under the Japanese during World War II and above all the overpowering importance of phosphate – all these helped destroy old Nauruan ways. Furthermore, royalties from the phosphate to the islanders themselves were often paltry, though the big company said they were ample for people who lived on 'coconuts and sunshine'.

But independent Nauru now owns the phosphate, and is putting profits aside so that even if the crumbly substance does run out in 1992, the islanders will be able to live on the investments. The generous spirit of *bubutsi* – if you admire something, the owner presents it to you – persists, but in matters of sheer survival, Nauruans have come to terms with the rest of the world.

(Top) High-ups discuss the question that all Nauruans ask: what will happen in 1992 when the phosphate runs out?

Phosphate gives Nauru the world's highest income per head, but bulldozers make rubble out of the island's center.

Nauruans are now expensively educated. The old culture is lost. But they enjoy ancient pastimes – like fishing for yellowtail and tuna.

13

Glossary to the peoples of the Pacific islands

The broad division of the Pacific peoples into three groups – the Polynesian, the Melanesian and the Micronesian – gives few clues to their origins. Some speculations are wild and imaginative: that the islands are remnants of a sunken continent. Others propose migrations from as far as South America. The evidence of archaeology, anthropology, botany and linguistics is not yet decisive; only occasionally do pieces appear to fall into place, to present a still incomplete picture.

Even the broad classifications of Pacific people hardly bears scrutiny. On Fiji the negroid Melanesian world intrudes upon the Polynesian. In Micronesia, the islanders in the eastern part are unlike those in the west who, in appearance, are closer to Indonesians. Everywhere in the Pacific there is this same confusion of physical and cultural traits, obscuring the identity of pre-historic strains. Polynesians are often classified as tall, light-skinned people with almost caucasoid features; but many have stocky, darker mongoloid features; with an epicanthic fold above the eye; among most there is a tendency to corpulence in middle age. None of the groups is a pure racial type; they all show extensive variations in all the physical and cultural features.

The link between a certain physical trait and a place of origin is hard to find. Almost 200 years of contact with Europeans has introduced a new strain into the already mixed population; and the far-reaching expeditions of many islanders can hardly have failed to permit inter-marriage. But the ruins of ancient buildings and other cultural artifacts tell much of the islanders' forbears although the diversity of objects, and the range of possible source areas, introduce further problems for the archaeologist. Peru, north-west America, south-east Asia, Japan, India and even China have all been cited as having cultural affinities with Polynesia. Heyerdahl's proposition that Peruvians sailed and drifted to Easter Island (see pages 94-101) is no longer in dispute; but as yet the theory that they went further into Polynesia or Micronesia is unproven. In time, no doubt archaeologists will unearth the secrets and tell in what sequence artifacts arrived, whether they were local or introduced, and thus explain the origins and migrations of the people who brought or invented them.

The most probable route of migration of the first Pacific peoples is from Indonesia. From there a great variety of people dispersed whether because of wars or through accidental voyages when their boats drifted onto currents which carried them hundreds of miles to sandy atolls or green islands. The Melanesian negritos are probably vestiges of these pre-historic settlers.

The Polynesians probably came by a most northerly route – by way of the Micronesian islands – from the south-east Asian mainland. The presence in Polynesia of certain plants – yams, taro and breadfruit – all Asian flora, indicate that this is almost certain. From the Society (Tahiti) and Marquesas Islands, in Polynesia, there were further migrations. Whether accidentally or because of wars, Polynesian people arrived in Hawaii in the north, and New Zealand in the south-west (as Maoris).

The evidence of plants, certain physical characteristics and cultural objects like outrigger canoes, all suggest an Asiatic origin for the Polynesian peoples. But the sweet potato presents a piece of botanical evidence that is intriguing. The sweet potato is native to South America, but common in Polynesia; in the Quechuan language (the language of the Incas) the word for the plant is similar to the Polynesian word for it. However, other words in the two languages are not alike and this suggests that the sweet potato and the word for it were introduced into the Pacific islands when they were already inhabited by a non-American people. We may suppose that occasional reed boats or balsa rafts did arrive in Polynesia from the east, but the weight of evidence points towards mass migrations from the west.

In the Micronesian islands where the people are apparently more mongoloid than their Polynesian neighbors to the south, there is a further confusion from the people's own origin myths. Their ancestral heroes were, according to tradition, fair-skinned like Europeans. They sprang from the branches and roots of a single ancestral tree; they had red complexions and blue eyes and were called the 'Company of the Tree, the Breed of Matang'. From them many of the islanders claim descent in the male line. The Land of Matang, where their ancestors dwelt eternally, was the land of heart's desire, the original fatherland. A tradition says that although Matang was lost forever, one of the ancestors, Au of the Rising Sun, had promised to return to his children one day. So, when white men were first seen by the islanders almost 200 years ago, the people said 'Behold, the Breed of Matang is returned to us.'

It is always difficult to assess the significance of traditions and origin myths, and in the case of the Pacific islands and the origins of the people, some point to a pre-historic dispersal from the west, while others point to ancestors of unknown origin. Often the myths confuse the issue even further. Any solution must at present be tentative; the answers can only come from wide research into linguistics, physical anthropology and archaeology.

There are many, often large, minorities of people in the Pacific islands who are quite distinct from the Polynesians, Melanesians and Micronesians. Indians and Chinese often came as laborers to work on plantations or in mines. The Japanese came in time of war, and many stayed. British, French and Americans have established themselves, often as administrators of the islands, most of which at some time have been under colonial rule.

AUSTRAL ISLANDS (TUBUAI ISLANDS) *Population:* 6,000. Languages: Polynesian, French. Area: 70 square miles. French Overseas Territory. The Austral or Tubuai Islands lie south of Tahiti in the south Pacific. Rapa and Marotiri (Bass) are south-east of the five main islands of which Tubuai is the capital. The islanders are Polynesians who probably came from the Society Islands in the north. They live largely by fishing and cultivating many crops, including 16 varieties of taro and 12 kinds of bananas. Some still engage in the traditional crafts of making canoes and weaving pandanus leaves for mats and building materials. They export copra, coffee, and cattle. On Raivavae and Rapa are stone statues resembling those on Easter Island. The *HMS Bounty* crew landed on Tubuai only to be driven back to Tahiti. They were attracted by Tubuai's luxuriant vegetation, mild climate and beautiful women.

AMERICAN SAMOA (see SAMOA)

BANABA (see OCEAN ISLAND)

BONIN ISLANDS *Population:* 250. Language: Japanese. Area: 27 square miles. Japanese territory. The Bonins lie 500 miles south-east of the Japanese mainland, north of the Volcano Islands in the western Pacific. There are three groups extending over 85 miles: the Mukoshima, Chichishima, and Hahashima, of which only Chichishima is inhabited. The islanders who live by subsistence fishing are descendants of original colonists who settled from 1830 onwards, a mixture of Japanese, European and American. US Trust Territories since World War II the islands were returned to Japan in 1968.

CAMPBELL ISLAND *Population:* 5. Language: English. Area: 44 square miles. New Zealand territory. There is one main island and several rocks peopled by the staff of a New Zealand weather station. It lies in the South Pacific 370 miles south by east of Stewart Island. There is a legend that a French princess, who was involved in a plot to restore the French monarchy, was abandoned here in the 1880s.

CAROLINE ISLANDS *Population:* 63,000. Languages: Micronesian, Polynesian, English. Area: 830 square miles. US Trust Territory. The 500 or more Caroline Islands which lie just north of the equator in the western Pacific are divided into five main groups: Palau (q.v.), Yap (q.v.), Truk (q.v.), Ponape (q.v.) and Kuaie (q.v.). The islanders are physically, culturally and linguistically very diverse. The islanders are Micronesians, although those in the western Carolines have intermarried with people from the Philippines. All have substantial elements of European, negro, and Japanese blood. Culturally they tend to be more Melanesian in the west and more Polynesian in the east. There are at least 12 separate languages and many dialects. Most islanders are subsistence farmers who grow a wide variety of root and tree crops, and raise livestock. Many also fish and collect trochus (mollusks with conical shells) and pearl shells from the ocean. Some work in bauxite mines on Babelthuag, Yap, Ponape, Kusaie, Angaur and Sonsorol. They construct the foundations of their houses, dancing platforms, and graves with stone, and elaborate stone causeways connect islets and cross bays on the high islands. On Yap, stone money is still regarded as the most stable currency – some of the stone coins are ten feet in diameter. The majority of Carolinians are Christian.
(pages 14-21)

CHATHAM ISLANDS *Population:* 500. Language: English. Area: 372 square miles. New Zealand territory. This small group of islands lies in the south Pacific, 450 miles east of South Island, New Zealand. There are three main islands, the largest of which is Whairikauri or Chatham Island. The original population of Moriori (physically different, but linguistically similar to the Maori) was practically exterminated in 1835 by a group of 800 New Zealand Maori, whose descendants now form half the population with Europeans who have lived here since 1840. The last pure Moriori died in 1933. The islanders now breed cattle and sheep, and export wool and fishery products, particularly frozen fish.

COOK ISLANDS *Population:* 22,000. Languages: Polynesian, English. Area: 93 square miles. Self-governing territory of New Zealand. The Cook Islands lie in the south Pacific 2,000 miles north-east of New Zealand. The larger islands of the southern group where

85 per cent of the population live, are high and fertile, and have as the main island, Rarotonga with a population of about 10,000, besides Mangaia, Mauke, Mitiaro, Manuae, Takutea, Atiu, Aitutaki. The northern group are smaller, sea level coral atolls: Tongareva, Manihiki, Rakahanga, Pukapuka, Nassau, Suvorov of which the best known of the group with a population of about 100 is Palmerston. The islanders, apart from about 300 Europeans, are Polynesians who are closely related in tradition, language, and custom to the New Zealand Maori. Rarotonga has several factories and a growing tourist industry. Most of the islanders are engaged in agriculture, copra-cutting, and fruit packing. The Cook Islands are named after Captain Cook who discovered them in 1773. For many years the Reverend John Williams of the London Missionary Society imposed a strict evangelical doctrine on the people and it is said that in no place in the world was the sabbath observed more vigorously than in the Cook Islands. Unoccupied until 1862, Palmerston Island became the home of an Englishman William Marsters, who took with him three Polynesian women. They became the forbears of a future population of over one hundred Marsters, more than seventy of whom still live on Palmerston, collecting pearl shells, drying fish and cutting copra, and speaking a strange 18th century English. An increasing number of Cook islanders migrate to New Zealand.

EASTER ISLAND *Population:* 1,200. Languages: Polynesian, Spanish. Area: 50 square miles. Dependency of Chile. Easter Island is the most easterly island of Polynesia; 2,230 miles from the South American coast and 1,100 miles east of Pitcairn. The indigenous islanders call it Te-Pito-te-Henua – the Navel of the Earth. Since slave-raiding, diseases, and wanton murder followed European discovery of the island in 1722 only about 200 people of pure Easter Island descent remain. They are believed by Thor Heyerdahl to originate from South America but may have come from the west. The rest of the islanders are the offspring of unions with Tahitians, Chileans, Tuamotuans, Europeans, Americans or Chinese. The islanders live in the village of Hanga Roa on the western side of the island. They are mostly small-scale farmers who grow corn, taro, yams and sweet potatoes. Some are employed by a sheep rearing concern, to which much of the island is leased. Now jet aeroplanes and tourists regularly visit the island. The native religion today is based on the Roman Catholic instruction of the early missionaries: virtually nothing is left of their

135

original Polynesian culture. However huge stone statues bear witness to the descendants of the pre-Inca Peruvian settlers on Easter Island; the largest weigh up to 50 tons. **(pages 94-101)**

ELLICE ISLANDS *Population:* 6,000. Languages: Polynesian, English. Area: 10 square miles. Part of Gilbert and Ellice Islands (q.v.) the Ellice Islands lie in the west Pacific to the south of the Gilberts. They consist of nine islands: Nanumea, Nanumanga, Niutao, Nui, Vaitupu, Nukufetau, Funafuti, Nukulaelae, Niulakita of which the best known is Funafuti. The islanders are a Polynesian people who live by simple agriculture and highly developed fishing techniques. They live in villages of native huts built of coconuts and pandanus timbers, and thatched with pandanus leaves. Each village has a large communal meeting house. The missionaries forbade old native customs, with the result that traditional dancing, music, and games – wrestling, foot racing, dart-throwing, and quarterstaff play – have practically died out on most of the islands. The islanders are predominantly Christian. **(pages 30-37)**

FIJI *Population:* 525,000. Languages: Melanesian, English. Area: 7,055 square miles. British Commonwealth nation. This large group of 325 islands lies in the south Pacific, 2,000 miles east of Australia and 3,200 miles south of Hawaii. It consists of the three large islands of Viti Levu (q.v.), Vanual Levu (q.v.) and Kandavu (q.v.), together with the Lomaiviti, Yasawa and Lau island groups. Only 105 of the islands are inhabited, but many more are used by Fijians for planting food crops or as temporary residences during the turtle fishing season. The 225,000 native Fijians, who are of mixed Melanesian and Polynesian stock, are outnumbered by 266,000 Indians. There are also about 6,000 Europeans, and the same number of Chinese, Rotumans, and other Pacific islanders. The indigenous Fijians are Christian, though taboos still prevail. For example, if you pluck a certain flower or mention a certain bird, you might be assaulted. The Indians are either Hindu or Muslim. Most Fijians live a communal village life on land they themselves own. Many work in the sugar or gold industries. The Indians laid the foundations of the sugar industry, and today grow most of the cane and supply the labor force in the crushing mills. They provide the bulk of the urban population, and

are busy artisans and shopkeepers. Some islanders are engaged in the rapidly-developing tourist industry. Fiji now has 90,000 visitors each year. **(pages 84-93)**

FOTUHA'A (see HA'APAI ISLANDS)

FRENCH OCEANIA *Population:* 100,000. Languages: Polynesian, French. Area: 1,500 square miles. French Overseas Territory. The Society Islands and the groups of islands immediately to the north-east, east and south of them comprise the political area known as the French Establishments in Oceania. (The title does not include all French possessions in the Pacific.) It comprises the Society (q.v.), Austral (q.v.) and Cambier (q.v.) Islands, the Marquesas (q.v.) together with Rapa and Marotiri. Most of the islands are small and are administered from Papeete in the Society Islands. The majority of the people are Polynesian or part-Polynesian. About 10 per cent are Chinese, and about 3 per cent European and American. French influence and culture are dominant among the Europeans and have spread to a considerable extent through the native population.

FUTUNA *Population:* 3,000. Languages: Polynesian, French. Area: 38 square miles. French Overseas Territory. Futuna lies between Fiji and West Samoa in the south Pacific. With its small neighbor Alofi, now uninhabited, they are sometimes known as the Horn (or Hoorn) Islands. The population consists almost exclusively of the indigenous islanders: Polynesians who came to the island from Samoa perhaps over 1,000 years ago. Most are still subsistence farmers growing taro and breadfruit, and maintaining small coconut plantations. They keep a few pigs, dogs and fowl. They also grow their own tobacco leaf, which they prefer to any imported tobacco. They used stone freely, but without cutting or trimming it, to line irrigation ditches and to face house platforms, burial mounds, and dams.

GALAPAGOS *Population:* 1,500. Language: Spanish. Area: 3,000 square miles. Province of Ecuador. This group of islands lies in the eastern Pacific near the equator 600–750 miles west of Ecuador. It consists of 13 islands, and a number of islets and rocks. The chief islands are Floreana and Santa Cruz. When discovered by the Spanish in the 16th century they were uninhabited, and not until the 20th century did sporadic settlement by Europeans begin, mainly on Santa Cruz and Floreana. In 1924, 200 Norwegians settled on Santa Cruz. Ecuadorans and French also settled on the islands. The people live in tiny villages of huts roofed with thatch or sheet iron, near their small plantations of sweet potatoes, sugar-cane, and bananas. Most grow enough food for themselves, fish and raise animals and export salt and sulphur. The majority are nominally Roman Catholic. The Spanish word 'Galapago' means tortoise and refers to the giant forms found here. They reached more than four feet in length, weighing over 500 pounds, and some lived for more than 200 years. These, like the large iguanas, are peculiar to the islands, which are visited by many scientific expeditions.

GAMBIER ISLANDS *Population:* 1,000. Languages: Polynesian, French. Area: 11 square miles. French Overseas Territory. The Gambier Islands (sometimes called the Forgotten Islands) are a small chain lying in the central Pacific about 900 miles south-east of Tahiti. The capital and most famous island is Mangareva, four miles long and about one mile wide. The earliest settlers on Mangareva were small numbers of Polynesian drift

voyagers from the Tuamotu islands (q.v.) and later from Rarotonga and the Marquesas (q.v.). Living chiefly on Mangareva itself, the present-day population of subsistence farmers cultivate breadfruit as a staple. Fish is an essential item of diet, its importance illustrated in the native saying that 'the sea is the garden of the poor.' There is also some pearl-shell diving. Most islanders are Christian, due to a strange episode in the last century. Père de Laval, a religious fanatic, engineer and architect took it upon himself to build a religious city on Mangareva. Five thousand Mangarevans died in the process. When Laval was called to account for his actions by the French Governor, he remarked 'True, Monsieur le Comte, but they have gone to heaven more quickly.' The islanders were drastically depleted in numbers. They have a carefree attitude towards work now: always *'ari'ana'* (by and by) will do.

GILBERT ISLANDS *Population:* 40,000. Languages: Micronesian, English. Area: 150 square miles. British colony. The Gilbert Islands straddle the equator south of the Marshalls in the central Pacific. They consist of 16 coral islands which vary from a few miles to about 30 miles in length and 100 yards to one mile in width. All the islands are inhabited: Tarawa, for example, has a population of 8,000, while Aranuak has only 600. The islanders are largely of Micronesian origin. The 'people of Makin' (of the north) have a long history of expansionist autocratic monarchies like those in the Marshalls. The

'people of Beru' (of the south) who have more democratic village councils and social organization are culturally more Polynesian. Many Gilbertese are fishermen. Most are subsistence farmers who grow coconut, pandanus, and breadfruit, and preserve and store surpluses in preparation for food shortages, particularly during droughts. They make *kamaimai*, a syrup derived from boiling coconut toddy, which they store in glass bottles obtained from Ocean Island or Nauru. They sell copra and handicrafts, especially pandanus mats. Some are laborers on Ocean Island (q.v.) and Nauru (q.v.). Their traditional technology persists in their plank sailing canoes and their large communal houses. Gilbertese delight in giving generously – particularly if the gifts are exhibited so that it becomes known that the donor is hard-working and humble. The majority of islanders are Christian.
(pages 30-37)

GUAM *Population:* 87,000. Languages: English, Chamorro. Area: 209 square miles. Unincorporated US Territory. Guam, the southernmost and largest of the Mariana Islands (q.v.) is in the west Pacific about 1,500 miles south-east of Manila in the Philippines. The original inhabitants were the Chamorros, a race of mongoloid stock, but of obscure origin who are now completely intermixed with Spanish and Filipinos (Tagalog). Only the Chamorro language now survives. Since the development of the island as a US military base which has brought an influx of 40,000 servicemen and their dependants the people have become highly westernized. Many work for wages paid by the US government. Others cultivate small plots of corn, vegetables and fruit, and raise a few chickens. Although they fish on the reef with spears, nets, and by making weirs they underexploit the ocean's resources. Many also now cater for the increasing numbers of tourists. They are predominantly Roman Catholic and maintain the west Pacific habit of chewing the narcotic betel nut with a pepper leaf and lime.

HA'APAI ISLANDS *Population₁* 19,000. Language: Polynesian. Area: 50 square miles. Part of Tonga (q.v.). This scattered archipelago of small islands consists of the three major islands of Lifuka, Foa, and Ha'ano, together with Uiha, Uoleva, Ofolanca, Mo'unga'one, Niniva, Lofanga, Fotuha'a, the Nomuka group, Ofo Tolu, the Kotu group, Late and Kao. They are mostly low, flat-topped, and wooded. The Polynesian

Tongans who inhabit the islands are mostly peasant farmers but also skilful navigators and fishermen. Although most of their traditional customs have lapsed they make clothes, bedding and room-dividers in the traditional way from tapa from the paper mulberry tree. Since Taufa'ahau, a former chief of Na'apai, was baptized in 1831 by the Wesleyan mission nearly all the islanders have become Free Wesleyans.

HAWAIIAN ISLANDS *Population:* 770,000. Languages: English, Polynesian. Area: 6,445 square miles. 50th State of the USA. The Hawaiian or Sandwich Islands are spread over an oceanic arc some 400 miles long near the center of the north Pacific Ocean. The eight major inhabited islands to the east are the Windwards; the smaller islands with few inhabitants, to the west, are the Leewards. The islands have been called a racial melting pot. The pure Hawaiians (Kanaka-natives), now numbering only 11,000 are Polynesians who came to the islands perhaps 1,000 to 1,500 years ago. Although they introduced all the food crops and the pig, most of the land which now grows sugar and pineapples was forest-covered and uncultivated. Americans and Europeans now numbering 205,000 came first as missionaries and traders. Their descendants, along with more recent immigrants manage the plantations, big ranches, banks, factories, mills, and large mercantile establishments. The need for laborers on the sugar plantations accounts for most of the immigration of Chinese (40,000), Japanese (205,000), and Filipino (70,000) who now operate small farms and retail stores, and work in clerical or professional occupations. There are also 95,000 of mixed blood and about 5,000 negroes. Little remains of Hawaiian native culture. Although hula performances proliferate exhibitions of the ancient hula, the sacred dance and chant of pre-discovery Hawaii, are increasingly rare. Independent native chieftains waged war on the islands until King Kamehameha I founded a dynasty in 1795 which reigned until US annexation in 1898.
(pages 62-73)

JUAN FERNANDEZ *Population:* 500. Language: Spanish. Area: 100 square miles. Territory of Chile. This small group of islands lies off the Chilean coast in the eastern Pacific some 360 miles west of Valparaiso. The two principal islands are Más-á-Tierra and Más-Afuera. Uninhabited when discovered in the

13

16th century, they were subsequently settled by Chilean Indians, and a trade in elephant seal's oil and bacalao (dried fish) was carried on. Alexander Selkirk was landed on Más-á-Tierra at his own request in 1704 and remained there until the next ship called in 1709, inspiring Daniel Defoe's novel *Robinson Crusoe*. The islanders are largely confined to the settlement in Cumberland Bay on Más-á-Tierra. They are predominantly Chilean, speak a corrupt form of Spanish and are mainly Roman Catholic. They fish, chiefly for a kind of lobster; some work in the canning factories and they grow fruit and vegetables for local consumption and raise small herds of cattle in some of the valleys.
(pages 112-117)

KANDAVU *Population:* 20,000. Languages: Melanesian, English. Area: 184 square miles. Part of Fiji (q.v.) Kandavu, is Fiji's third largest island and lies about 50 miles south of Viti Levu. The Fijian inhabitants, of mixed Melanesian-Polynesian origin, are mostly subsistence farmers and live in villages predominantly along the coast where they grow taro, yams, breadfruit and 30 varieties of bananas, and prepare and sell copra. The economy is less developed on Kandavu than on other Fijian islands.

KAO (see HA'APAI ISLANDS)

KOTU ISLANDS (see HA'APAI ISLANDS)

KUSAIE *Population:* 1,800. Languages: Micronesian, Polynesian, English. Area: 60 square miles. Part of Caroline Islands group (q.v.) Kusaie and its neighbor Lele are fringed by eight low coral reefs and lie 307 miles from Ponape (q.v.) at the easternmost end of the Caroline Island chain (q.v.). It has a fine climate, luxuriant vegetation and has been famed for well over a century for the further education available to people from all over Micronesia at its educational center. Most of Kusaie's inhabitants live in the small coastal villages and in the main valley in the center of the island.

KERMADEC ISLANDS *Population:* 9. Language: English. Area: 13 square miles. New Zealand Territory. This small group lies about 600 miles north-east of Auckland, New Zealand. There are five islands, of which Raoul is the largest and inhabited by nine government radio and meterorological officers. Although Polynesian voyagers came, stayed and left behind various stone artifacts on the islands in the past, later attempts to settle here were unsuccessful.

LATE (see HA'APAI ISLANDS)

LINE ISLANDS *Population:* 600. Language: English. Area: 200 square miles. The Line Islands chain straddles the equator in the central Pacific. Washington, Fanning and Christmas islands in the north form the Line Islands District of the Gilbert and Ellice Islands Colony (q.v.). Although since their discovery by Europeans in the 18th century the Line Islands have had no permanent population, stone ruins and temple buildings on Fanning and Christmas Island suggest that there was once a sizeable population. On Christmas Island, the largest coral atoll in the Pacific, the British government authorized H-bomb tests to be carried out. Before trans-Pacific aviation and nuclear weapon tests Line Islands main importance derived from its large guano deposits. Later coconut plantations were developed.

LOFANGA (see HA'APAI ISLANDS)

LOMAIVITI ISLANDS *Population:* 18,000. Languages: Melanesian, English. Area: 158 square miles. Part of Fiji (q.v.). These islands lie in the Koro sea. The islanders of mixed Melanesian-Polynesian origin, are mostly subsistence peasant farmers who make copra for sale as well as a variety of tropical food crops. There are fewer Indians here than on the major islands. Makongai island is famous for its leprosy hospital which serves a large area of the south Pacific.

LAU ISLANDS *Population:* 15,000. Languages: Melanesian, English. Area: 188 square miles. Part of Fiji (q.v.). In this easternmost group of the Fiji archipelago

the islands are small and isolated, and have as their leading island Lakemba. It is in this group of islands that the Polynesian influences are strongest in the mixed Melanesian-Polynesian make-up of the Fijians. Here Tongan influence, prevalent throughout the Fiji archipelago a hundred years ago, has remained strongest. The Lau group was the source of great canoes highly prized by the Tongans. The islanders today are mostly subsistence peasant farmers, growing a variety of tropical food crops and a little copra for sale. They are predomiantly Christian.

LELE (see KUSAIE, CAROLINE ISLANDS)

MANGAREVA (see GAMBIER ISLANDS)

LORD HOWE ISLAND *Population:* 250. Language: English. Area: 4½ square miles. Australian Territory. This small island lies in the west Pacific about halfway between Norfolk Island and Sydney, Australia. The inhabitants are descendants of Sydney-siders who squatted on the island 100 years ago, and still squat rent-free on Crown land on sufferance. They produce seed for export from the indigenous Kentia palm, fish, cater for a small tourist trade and cultivate their land.

MAKONGAI (see LOMAIVITI ISLANDS)

MARIANA ISLANDS *Population:* 13,000. Languages: Micronesian, English. Area: 400 square miles. US Trust Territory. This group of islands lies north of Guam (q.v.) in the west Pacific and stretches northward to include Farallon de Pajaros. The other main islands are Saipan – the most highly populated – Rota and Tinian. Discovered by Magellan in 1521 the Marianas were then occupied by the Chamorros, a race of obscure mongoloid stock, who had come there perhaps from the Malay area. The Chamorros, who have died out, left in the islands neolithic stone tools, bone implements and the latte: double rows of capped pillars believed to have served as supports for houses and canoe sheds. Otherwise the islanders are of mixed descent: chiefly Spanish and Filipino, but also German, Japanese and American. Although some indigenous culture, like the language, has persisted, it is mainly intermixed with Spanish culture. They are subsistence cultivators and earn cash from copra-drying.

MARQUESAS ISLANDS *Population:* 5,000. Languages: Polynesian, French. Area: 410 square miles. French Overseas Territory. The ten chief islands of the Marquesas lie north of the Tuamotu archipelago (q.v.) in the central Pacific. The most important island is Nuku Hiva. The Marquesans are Polynesians similar to the Maori of New Zealand. Numbering perhaps 50,000 at the beginning of the 19th century, they were reduced by veneral disease, tuberculosis, leprosy, alcohol, and opium (all introduced by Europeans) to about 2,000 within a hundred years. Now they are a shadow of the mighty people they once were. They offered fierce resistance to an American force which first tried to conquer them, and were only overcome by cannons. They are subsistence farmers, who raise a few cattle and grow coffee, vanilla, and copra for cash. Their only other sources of cash are selling services and wood carvings to tourists. Marquesan women scour the seaside rock ledges and boulders for shellfish which like all fish they eat raw. The Marquesans have a tradition of highly developed arts and crafts using elaborate geometrical designs in wood carving and tattooing: tattoo artists still live on the more isolated island of Fatuhiava. An elected chief presides over each valley, formerly the home of a separate tribe. The

Marquesas are known as the Spain of Polynesia and the islanders are Catholics. It seems certain that migrants from this group of islands went to Easter Island and Hawaii. In one valley Gauguin, who immortalized the spirit of the Marquesans in his paintings, died in abject poverty and great pain. He went there from Tahiti and claimed he had come 10,000 miles to find freedom. In his novel *Typee Valley* Melville recreates the Marquesans as they were a century ago.

MARSHALL ISLANDS *Population:* 23,000. Languages: Micronesian, English. Area: 70 square miles. US Trust Territory. The Marshall Islands lie in the west Pacific, northwest of the Gilbert Islands. Two separate chains of atolls run north-west to south-east. The more westerly is the Ralik (sunset) chain; the other, the Ratak (sunrise) chain. The Marshallese are Micronesians, regarded as among the primitive world's best fishermen who skilfully exploit the many resources of the ocean with a score of devices, including the spear, line, trap and net. Most of the islanders are subsistence farmers and are predominantly Christian. Although stratified groups of nobility and commoners still persist in some atolls, they can no longer be distinguished by dress, diet or behavior. Bikini and Eniwetok became centers for atomic bomb experiments and the inhabitants were transferred to other islands. Those from Eniwetok are now in the process of attempting to return to their island.
(pages 22-29)

MELANESIA *Population:* 3 million. Languages: Melanesian, French, English, Dutch. Area: 400,000 square miles. This is one of the three principal ethnological divisions of the Pacific Islands, the other two being Polynesia (q.v.) and Micronesia (q.v.). It consists of the huge island of New Guinea, the great Bismarck archipelago, the Solomons and New Hebrides, running eastward to New Caledonia and Fiji. 2½ million of the total population are indigenous to the islands and are of predominantly negroid stock. In speech, custom and acclimatization to western civilization Melanesians differ vastly from one community to the next. In eastern Melanesia the Fijians and New Caledonians are nearly all Christian, while in the west many remote tribes still remain virtually unaffected by European influences. The majority are subsistence small-holders who keep pigs and cultivate taro and yams as staples.

MICRONESIA *Population:* 220,000. Languages: Micronesian, English. Area: 1,200 square miles. With Melanesia (Volume I) and Polynesia (q.v.) Micronesia is one of the three principal ethnological divisions of the Pacific. Islands of the Micronesian group include over 2,000 small coral atoll islands most of which lie north of the equator including the Carolines (q.v.), Marshalls (q.v.), Marianas (q.v.) including Guam (q.v.), Gilberts (q.v.), and Nawa (q.v.). The Micronesians tend to be short and slight, copper-colored, thin-lipped and have straight black hair; they are physically heterogeneous. Micronesia is defined as a distinct cultural area by the presence in the societies of a clan system, in which a totem is assigned to each clan; religions which revere both heavenly creators and ancestral spirits; and the relics of an early megalithic culture not found elsewhere in Oceania. Like the Polynesians, these islanders are seafarers, and win a large part of their livelihood from the ocean. They are particularly skilled in weaving and basketry. The majority are now Christian – mainly Roman Catholic in the west, where Spanish missionaries have been at work since the late 16th century, and Protestant in the east, where American and British missions came nearly three centuries later.

MO'UNGA'ONE (see HA'APAI ISLANDS)

NAURU *Population:* 6,700. Language: Nauruan. Area: 81 square miles. Independent state. Nauru lies in the west Pacific just south of the equator and nearly 400 miles west of the Gilbert Islands. The 3,400 native Nauruans are a mixture of Polynesian, Micronesian, and Melanesian. They speak a language distinct from the other great Pacific language groups. The island's only resources are the renowned high-grade phosphate deposits. Exported to Australia and New Zealand, they have made the islanders very prosperous: Nauru has the world's highest per capita income. The deposits have also brought newcomers: nearly 1,000 Chinese mostly as laborers, housed in barracks; and some 600 Europeans. When they achieved independence in 1968, the native Nauruans elected to remain on the island in future rather than follow an earlier plan to transfer them to another island when the phosphate deposits become exhausted.
(pages 132-133)

NEW ZEALAND *Population:* 2,860,000. Language: English. Area: 103,740 square miles. Dominion of the British Commonwealth. New Zealand lies in the south-west Pacific about 1,500 miles south-east of Sydney, Australia. North Island (44,300 square miles) is separated by the narrow Cook strait from South Island (59,440 square miles). The population, mostly of European (particularly British) descent, also includes 170,000 native Maori and 15,000 Polynesians, all unevenly distributed: while North Island has 2,051,000 people, the mountainous South Island has only 809,000 inhabitants. The European settlers came late in the 18th century, bought land from the indigenous Maori and established a society dependent upon agricultural resources and overseas markets.
(pages 118-131)

NINIVA (see HA'APAI ISLANDS)

NIUE *Population:* 5,300. Language: Polynesian. Area: 100 square miles. Territory of New Zealand. Niue is in the south Pacific between the Tongan and Cook islands. The Niueans are Polynesians thought to have come from Tonga and Samoa at least 1,000 years ago. The hostile reception they gave Captain Cook caused him to call Niue Savage Island. In 1861 Peruvian slavers carried off several hundred islanders. Although water is scarce and there are frequent droughts they practise forestry and subsistence farming, raise livestock and export some copra. They manufacture and export plaited mats and other objects to New Zealand (q.v.).

NOMUKA ISLANDS (see HA'APAI ISLANDS)

OCEAN ISLAND (BANABA) *Population:* 2,500. Languages: Micronesian, English. Area: 2 square miles. Part of Gilbert and Ellice Islands (q.v.). Ocean Island lies in the west Pacific some 250 miles west of the Gilbert Islands. Like Nauru (q.v.) the island is a raised coral atoll, with valuable phosphate deposits. The indigenous Banabans were resettled on Rabi Island (Fiji) in 1945. The present population includes several hundred Europeans and Chinese, who mostly mine phosphates.

OFOLANCA (see HA'APAI ISLANDS)

OFU TOLU (see HA'APAI ISLANDS)

PALAU ISLANDS *Population:* 1,200. Languages: Micronesian, English. Area: 200 square miles. Part of Caroline Islands (q.v.) this compact group of about 200 islands lies in the south-western Carolines in the west Pacific. Most of the native Micronesians live on Babelthuap. They are predominantly subsistence farmers and fishermen, who also grow coconuts for copra. At present they are being encouraged to improve their agricultural production. Phosphate was mined on Angaur and Peleliu until 1955. While the islanders were mandated to Japan (1920–1945) pineapples for canning and cassava were introduced to the islands. They are the most sophisticated of the Caroline islanders chiefly due to their close contact with the Japanese.

PHOENIX ISLANDS *Population:* 2,500. Languages: Polynesian, English. Area: 18 square miles. Part of Gilbert and Ellice Islands except for Canton and Enderbury Islands, jointly administered by US-UK Condominium. These eight small scattered islands lie north of the Tokelau Islands in the central Pacific. The islands were largely uninhabited until developed as bases for trans-Pacific commercial air routes. Canton has an international airport for flights between Fiji and Honolulu, and has a hundred or so European inhabitants. Surplus population from the southern Gilbert Islands was resettled on Hull, Sydney and Gardner between 1938 and 1940 under a planned colonization scheme. The islanders have a subsistence economy but also produce copra for cash from specially introduced coconut trees. Most of the islands yielded guano phosphate in the past.

PITCAIRN ISLANDS *Population:* 80. Language: English dialect. Area: 2 square miles. British colony. The islands of Pitcairn with Oeno, Henderson and Ducie which lie in the central Pacific to the south-east of the Tuamotu archipelago are, together with Easter Island (q.v.) the only substantial bits of land in the entire western half of the Pacific. The islanders who are descendants of the nine *HMS Bounty* mutineers, six Tahitian men and twelve Tahitian women, who settled on Pitcairn in 1790, have an English-Tahitian culture. Tahitian cultural elements include the five-pronged fishing spear, torch for fishing, light fishing canoe, and the *pilihai* pudding made from sweet potatoes or taro and coconut cream. The people are farmers, fishermen or craftsmen, and have a single

settlement, Adamstown, of about 60 simple unpainted houses. They make large boats of the whaleboat variety and the women plait hats and baskets of pandanus leaves. Pitcairn men have recently taken temporary work in New Zealand. Seventh Day Adventists since 1886, they are primarily vegetarians.
(pages 102-111)

POLYNESIA *Population:* 3,785,000. Languages: Polynesian, English. Area: 114,000 square miles. The Polynesian group of islands cover a vastly larger area than the other two principal ethnological divisions of the Pacific Islands: Micronesia (q.v.) and Melanesia (q.v. and Volume I). The area includes the two islands of New Zealand; the Tuamotu (q.v.) and Wallis (q.v.) archipelago; the Line (q.v.), Cook (q.v.), Ellice (q.v.), Phoenix (q.v.), Tokelau (q.v.), Tonga (q.v.), Marquesas (q.v.), Society (q.v.), and Austral (Tubuai) islands and extends north to include Hawaii (q.v.) and east as far as Easter Island (q.v.); and also includes part of the Samoan archipelago (q.v.). The Polynesians are regarded as culturally more advanced, and appear caucasian compared with the negroid Melanesians. They are good natural sailors, divers, and fishermen, and have been called the Vikings of the Pacific. They are thought to have migrated in successive waves through Micronesia from south-east Asia. They overcame a lack of iron by their ingenuity in making knives of bamboo, shark's teeth, and shells; hatchets out of stone; fish hooks out of bone and spears out of wood. Although each island group has developed cultural differences, the Polynesians are similar in their language, fishing methods, and in their aristocratic social system by which high chiefs trace their descent directly back to the gods. Little survives of indigenous Polynesian religion, as by the end of the 19th century nearly all the Polynesians were converted to Christianity.

PONAPE ISLANDS *Population:* 24,000. Languages: Polynesian, English. Area: 176 square miles. Part of the Caroline Islands (q.v.). The islands of the Ponape group lie 900 to 1,200 miles south and east of Guam and are a west Pacific group of the Caroline Islands. The islanders, apart from the inhabitants of Kapingamarangi and Nukuoro who are partly Polynesian, are mainly of Melanesian stock. The higher islands have been centers of trade and cultural influence since prehistoric times. The islanders are fishermen and farmers or small-holders, who grow bread-fruit, cassava, root crops, and kava. They compete to produce prize tropical yams, kava plants and pigs in return for honorary titles and the accompanying prestige and advancement. They enjoy eating dogs, especially at ceremonies. On Ngalik the islanders also occasionally eat cats. The islanders of Kapingamarangi catch sharks by pulling them up by a rope from their canoes and then clubbing them to death. Most of the islanders are Christians.

ROTUMA *Population:* 3,500. Language: Polynesian. Dependency of Fiji (q.v.). Area: 18 square miles. The island is isolated in the south Pacific some 300 miles north of the Fiji group. The Polynesian Rotumans are a prosperous people who have been getting cash from exporting copra for many years. They grow a few food crops and catch a huge variety of fish on the reefs and in the surrounding waters. There is a large Rotuman community in Fiji (q.v.) with whom they maintain close ties: every adult Rotuman endeavors to visit Fiji at least once. They play the traditional sports of *tika* (dart throwing) and *hula* (wrestling); the vast majority of the population tends to turn up to formal matches. Their supreme deity used to be Tangaroa, incarnate in a turtle. Now, because of missionary teaching, the people on one side of the island are Methodist and those on the other side, Roman Catholic.

SAMOA ISLANDS *Population:* 160,000. Languages: Polynesian, English. Area: 1,176 square miles. American Samoa: Unincorporated US Territory – Western Samoa: British Commonwealth Nation. The Samoa chain of islands, nine of which are inhabited, stretches for 290 miles in the south Pacific some 750 miles west of Tahiti. Like the Tongans, the Polynesian Samoans have lived for so long on their islands that they have no clear memory of their ancestors' pioneering voyages, which are hinted at in legends. 30,000 Samoans live in New Zealand and the United States. The island Samoans are remarkably close-knit, and although an increasing number now work for wages, they remain smallholding farmers who occasionally fish. Although formerly all of a single aristocracy, the islands are today divided politically into Western Samoa (population: 132,000) which became independent from New Zealand in 1962, and of which the main island is Savai'i, and American Samoa (population: 28,000) which has as its main, most populated island, Tutuila. In Western Samoa the inhabitants live in the Polynesian tradition, by the coast, men wearing the Samoan *lavalava* wrapped around the lower part of their portly frames and maintaining their respect for traditional Samoan ceremony. They have a flourishing system of chiefships, based on an intricate hierarchy of graded titles. The *aiga,* the extended family, with the *Matai* as its elected titled head, is the basic unit of Samoan society. They are subsistence farmers and rear large herds of Hereford and Angus cattle. About half the islanders are members of the London Missionary Society. In American Samoa only the 3,500 inhabitants of the Manu's group of islands continue the indigenous way of life relatively free from disturbance. Elsewhere, American influence, subsidies and government employment have westernized the islanders, who derive a high standard of living from the US naval base at Pago Pago. They are frequently visited by relatives from Western Samoa.
(pages 44-53)

SANDWICH ISLANDS (see HAWAIIAN ISLANDS)

SOCIETY ISLANDS (see TAHITI)

STEWART ISLAND *Population:* 350. Language: English. Area: 670 square miles. New Zealand Territory. Stewart Island lies across Bluff Strait to the south of South Island, New Zealand. The inhabitants are of European, mostly British, descent. Some cater for the summer tourists from the mainland. Some depend wholly or partly on the fishing industry, the only surviving pioneering industry; sealing, whaling, mining, and timber milling have all gone. Oban, the only township, is a small collection of houses and cottages lost in wooded gardens up the slope at the head of Half Moon Bay. Since the early 19th century Stewart Island has remained the home of a few hardy settlers. Isolated and inaccessible, it is likely to remain a backwater.

TAHITI (SOCIETY ISLANDS) *Population:* 70,000. Languages: Polynesian, French. Area: 600 square miles. French Overseas

141

Territory. Part of French Oceania, the islands, now known as the Society Islands, lie in the central south Pacific to the south-west of the Tuamotu archipelago. The Windward group of islands includes Tahiti and Moorea as main islands and the Leeward group includes Raiatea, Borabora (reputedly the most beautiful island in the entire Pacific) and Maupik. The islands were possibly the center from which Polynesians spread throughout the Pacific and the indigenous islanders are Polynesian. About half the population of Tahiti island itself, the largest and most highly populated (55,000) of the entire group are Polynesian and probably came here from the Tahitian island of Raiatea; one quarter are French and of mixed blood; and there are ten thousand Chinese who are prominent as shopkeepers and market gardeners. The rest of the population grow crops, prepare copra for export, raise pigs and cattle and are increasingly involved in tourism. The island has been a mecca for authors and artists ever since Gauguin came here and immortalized the indigenous Polynesian life in his pictures. The indigenous culture is now progressively eroded by increasing contact with French and international tourist culture. The islanders of the group live principally by selling either their labor or the produce of their fishing and agriculture. They cultivate, with simple tools, taro, breadfruit, bananas, vanilla and prepare copra for export. Houses along the coasts of Tahiti and Moorea are built on the ground while those on most of the Leeward Islands are raised on platforms. Raiatea is important in Polynesian history and tradition, particularly for the prestige of its great temple Taputapuatea dedicated to Oro, the god of war, to whom human heads were offered. The island is also the home of a fire-walking cult, the *umuti* ceremony, which is still occasionally performed. The men of Borabora are skilled craftsmen; their large sailing canoes are famous for their grace of line and beauty of workmanship. Though all the islanders have been Christian for over a century, they are still often unwilling to set foot on a ruined temple site and most believe in the ghosts of the dead.
(pages 74-83)

TOKELAU ISLANDS *Population:* 2,000. Languages: Polynesian, English. Area: 4 square miles. New Zealand Territory. The three small Tokelau islands – Fakaofu, Nukunono and Atafu – lie in the South Pacific about 300 miles north of West Samoa. The islands have been invaded, since European discovery, by Polynesians from Samoa, with whom the Tokelauans retain linguistic and cultural ties. Their culture and economy are limited by their atoll environment: apart from a little sun-dried copra they raise only subsistence crops. They live in three villages in ordered rows of houses constructed of pandanus timbers with walls and roofs of woven pandanus fibers. The gabled roofs and occasional verandas indicate affinities with the Gilbert and Ellice islanders' (q.v.) houses. On Atafu and Fakaofu most inhabitants are members of the London Missionary Society, while on Nukunono they are all Roman Catholics. As the islands are densely populated and have only limited economic and social resources each year some of the population voluntarily resettle in New Zealand.

TONGA ISLANDS *Population:* 86,000. Languages: Polynesian, English. Area: 270 square miles. British Commonwealth Kingdom. The 150 islands of the Tonga group lie in the west Pacific south-east of Fiji and south-west of Samoa. There are three main island groups: Vava'u (q.v.), H'a'apai (q.v.) and Tongatapu (q.v.) and several outlying islands, the most important of which are Niuatoputapu (167 miles north of Vava'u) and Niuafo'ou – formerly known as Tin Can Island because the mail was sent ashore in sealed biscuit tins (211 miles north-west of Vava'u). The Tongans are a Polynesian people who once ruled an empire which included parts of Samoa, Fiji and Tahiti. They have preserved much of their traditional way of life and adopted only those European influences which they feel are compatible with it. The islanders are primarily landowning market gardeners who grow root crops, fruit and fibers, chiefly for their own family consumption. Until the mid-19th century the supreme chief was the Tu'i Tonga, a sacred King who was the highest representative of the gods on earth and to whom annual tribute was made on all the islands. Tongan social relations are dominated by a complex system of social rank. The kingdom achieved independence from Britain in 1970.
(pages 54-61)

TONGATAPU ISLANDS *Population:* 44,000. Languages: Polynesian, English. Area: 140 square miles. Part of Tonga (q.v.). This southernmost of the Tongan Island group (q.v.) includes the principal Tongan island of Tongatapu, which means 'Sacred Tonga' and has traditional importance as a center of religious and social life. The islanders who are not peasant farmers and fishermen work for wages in the chief port, whaling and urban center of Nuku'alofa on Tongatapu. Some native traditions still survive, such as the *ta'ovala,* the pandanus-leaf mat worn around the waist. But with the advent of tourism, the islanders are becoming more westernized. They are Christians, mostly members of the Free Wesleyan Church. A long history of shifting cultivation has destroyed the timber forests, except on Eua.

TRUK GROUP *Population:* 30,000. Languages: Polynesian, English. Area: 47 square miles. Part of Caroline Islands (q.v.). In the west Pacific 600 miles south and east of Guam, Truk contains several of the islands in the Truk group in its huge lagoon which is probably the largest in the world. The Trukese who are predominantly Micronesian inhabit most of the islands. The higher islands have been centers of trade and cultural influence since prehistoric times. The islanders have long been influenced by other cultures, particularly American and Japanese, although on Tol, the most densely populated of the islands, indigenous life has been less disturbed. Most islanders grow their own food: breadfruit, coconut, taro and bananas. On some islands they cultivate arrowroot, kava (a mild drug), and sugar cane. They are predominantly Christian, converts largely of American missionaries.

TUAMOTU ARCHIPELAGO *Population:* 9,000. Languages: Polynesian, French. Area: 330 square miles. French Overseas Territory. The 76 Tuamotu islands are a 900 miles long chain scattered from north-west to south-east over a huge area east of Tahiti in the central Pacific. The islanders who are Polynesians, still conscious of *ati,* membership of a descent group, have a largely subsistence economy based on coconut palms which provide materials for many sorts of construction, as well as food. They also cultivate taro and breadfruit on the more populous atolls and

rear few animals except pigs. The islands are the center of the French Oceanic pearlshell industry, and attract the best divers from all over French Oceania.

TUBUAI ISLANDS (see AUSTRAL ISLANDS)

UIHA (see HA'APAI ISLANDS)

UOLEVA (see HA'APAI ISLANDS)

USA TRUST TERRITORIES *Population:* 108,000. Languages: Micronesian, English. Area: 700 square miles. Trust territory of the United Nations. The Trust territories of America in the Pacific consist of the Mariana Islands (q.v.) (except Guam), the Carolines (q.v.) and the Marshalls (q.v.). The 2,141 islands, of which 90 are inhabited, are grouped into six administrative districts. The Trusteeship Agreement, approved by the United Nations in 1947, designated these islands as a strategic area and the United States as the Administering Authority of the

Territory. The inhabitants of the islands are Micronesians.

UVEA (see WALLIS ISLAND)

VANUA LEVU *Population:* 100,000. Languages: Melanesian, English. Area: 2,200 square miles. Part of Fiji (q.v.). Vanua Levu is the second largest island of the Fiji group where islanders who are of mixed Melanesian-Polynesian origin live the communal village life, growing various tropical crops, stock-raising, and preparing copra for sale. Others either work in the Vanua Levu gold mines or seek urban and factory employment here and on Viti Levu (q.v.).

VAVA'U ISLANDS *Population:* 19,000. Languages: Polynesian, English. Area: 56 square miles. Part of Tonga (q.v.) this group lies about 60 miles north-east of the Ha'apai (q.v.) group of Tongan islands and consists of Uta Vava'u and about 40 smaller islands around its southern end. They are high, flat-topped, and very fertile, although only half of them are inhabited. The Polynesian islanders are mostly peasant farmers, though fish is an important part of their diet. Each male Tongan at the age of 16 has the right to a plot of land *(api)* and a building site in a village. To keep his *api* he must pay rent and taxes, and have at least 200 coconut trees growing within the first year and produce sufficient food crops to feed a family. They are nearly all Christians, the majority members of the Free Wesleyan Church.

WALLIS ISLAND *Population:* 7,000. Language: Polynesian. Wallis Island, which is sometimes called Uvea, is French Overseas Territory and together with its twelve small surrounding islets is in the south Pacific between Fiji and West Samoa. Although the islanders bear traces of Melanesian stock, they are a Polynesian people. Their culture is essentially like that of the Tongans. They are predominantly subsistence farmers who grow taro, breadfruit, tapioca and bananas; and copra and trochus for export. They fish, raise pigs, cattle and horses and make tapa cloth from the paper mulberry. Of their native culture, only their language remains intact. Most are Roman Catholics.

143

YAP ISLANDS *Population:* 7,400. Languages: Micronesian, English. Area: 40 square miles. Part of Caroline Islands (q.v.). This group in the western Carolines lies in the west Pacific just north of the equator and has as its main island Yap. The Yapese have distinct linguistic and racial characteristics: there is a strong mixture of mongolian, Melanesian, and Polynesian blood. Local customs have restrained the indigenous islanders from mixing culturally, socially and sexually with Japanese and Americans as on other Caroline Islands. The islanders grow subsistence crops: yams, sweet potatoes, pepper, cloves, and tobacco and fish, and produce copra. The women make their own skirts – their only garments – of various grasses, leaves and long fibers. Men often wear only loin cloths. They have a caste system in which their villages are ranked. Most houses are made of wood, bamboo, and thatch. Ceremonial dancing still plays an important part in native life. **(pages 14-21)**

All population figures are approximate.